Does Your Man Have the Blues?

DR. DAVID HAWKINS

HARVEST HOUSE PUBLISHERS

EUGENE, OREGON

Cover by Koechel Peterson & Associates, Inc., Minneapolis, Minnesota

This book includes stories in which the author has changed people's names and some details of their situations to protect their privacy.

DOES YOUR MAN HAVE THE BLUES?
Copyright © 2004 by David Hawkins
Published by Harvest House Publishers
Eugene, Oregon 97402
www.harvesthousepublishers.com

Library of Congress Cataloging-in-Publication Data

Hawkins, David, 1951-
 Does your man have the blues? / David Hawkins.
   p. cm.
 ISBN 0-7369-1348-3 (pbk.)
 1. Depression in men—Religious aspects—Christianity. I. Title.
 BV4910.34.H38 2004
 248.8'625—dc22   2004005285

Printed in the United States of America

  04 05 06 07 08 09 10 11 / BP-MS / 10 9 8 7 6 5 4 3 2 1

This book is dedicated to the countless men who suffer silently from the ravages of depression, and to the women who stand by, encouraging but often feeling helpless. It is dedicated to those who struggle against the culture of silence and risk seeking help for their pain.

Acknowledgments

As I lean into the latter years of my counseling practice, I have a greater desire to share what I have learned. I enjoy sharing my understanding about people and relationships through my writing. Though it may appear to be a solo enterprise, it is anything but that. Many people have helped me craft my skills and share my experiences in such a way as to make them readable.

First, let me again thank the many men and women who have shared their stories with me. I never take their confidence in me for granted. It is a sacred trust. Their lives are interwoven in these pages, disguised of course, to protect that trust and preserve anonymity.

Again, I am grateful to the Harvest House family. As I travel extensively to share the stories in my books, I am always greeted warmly because of the Harvest House team of professionals that has gone before me to prepare the way. Thanks, folks. Let's keep it up.

A special thanks goes again to my "personal editor," Gene Skinner. He is a major voice behind mine that challenges and encourages me to say more clearly what I am really trying to say. He has tightened up the writing, making it sharper. I appreciate it so much. Thanks again, Gene. Will you stick with me for one more?

And again, I have my personal team of editors who always encourage my writing. They read what I have written, willingly, and are the first to tell me that I have something important to say. They encourage me but also, invariably, tell me that I can write better. And so I go back and edit. I don't always like their feedback, but it is always helpful. Thanks, Jim and Christie.

I must also again thank my parents, Hank and Rose Hawkins, for their constant encouragement. I could write poorly and they would still read it and say it was great. Thanks, Mom and Dad.

Finally, I thank my Lord Jesus, who blesses me beyond measure.

Contents

A Sure and Hidden Darkness: Bringing the Problem into the Light

Those who have crossed
With direct eyes, to death's other Kingdom
Remember us—if at all—not as lost
Violent souls, but only
As the hollow men
The stuffed men.

—T.S. ELIOT

I HAD A DISTINCT FEELING OF APPREHENSION as I approached the church. I slipped down the alley and pulled into the rear entrance of the parking lot. Coasting to a stop, almost as if I were involved in some sort of clandestine operation, I scanned the area to see if any other cars were nearby. None were present.

The skies were overcast on this November morning, a brooding harbinger of another dreary fall day. The month before, we had reluctantly said goodbye to our Indian summer with its delightful moonlit evenings and a wisp of chill in the air. We were moving headlong into the damp, dark season when my long wool overcoat is my constant companion.

I had invited several other men to join me for a men's support group this morning. Now the phrase felt like an oxymoron—*men's support group*. Who was I kidding? Would a group of men gather with me to share and explore their inner feelings and fears? I surely felt the need, but did others? In spite of the encouraging national response to Promise Keepers and its massive marketing campaign, I had concerns that men would not respond to my fledgling attempt to form a group to talk about feelings.

I entered the darkened church, passed the somber sanctuary, and made my way back to the pastor's office. At least he was there.

"Hey, Jim. Good to see you," I said.

"You, too," he said enthusiastically. "Think anybody else is going to make it?"

"Pat said he would be here. And Mike said he would try to make it. Terry said he would be here, but he didn't seem too excited."

"Well," Jim said reassuringly, "if it's just you and me, then we'll have one small, intimate group." The twinkle in his eyes was encouraging.

We laughed as we moved through this awkward moment. We both understood that starting a men's group would be difficult. Gathering men for anything other than a golf tournament was a major ordeal. We knew then what we still know now: Men hide their pain.

Of the five hopefuls, including myself, only three showed up that first morning. But three was enough to keep us from feeling awkward. Enough for us to legitimately call ourselves a group. Enough for us to agree to come back next week for another gathering.

I was both encouraged and discouraged by the results of that first meeting. I had been experiencing more than a little emotional turmoil in my life due to marital challenges and enormous work pressures. I had admitted that I was a bona fide workaholic and desperately needed support and encouragement as I tried to find balance in my life. I was searching, mostly in vain, for a role model who would show me how to be a man who was successful and enterprising, yet reflective and caring.

I needed this group. In spite of my training, I often felt ill equipped to manage my intense feelings of disappointment in my marriage. I knew how to talk to my spouse, but our resolve to improve things often slipped away. I blamed myself, I blamed her. I wanted to know if other men might be experiencing similar challenges.

In addition to typical marital issues, I struggled with a trait I inherited from my father, whom I so admire. I worked too hard. I still work too hard. At times I felt as if I had no governor on my engine, as if the accelerator was stuck and I couldn't find the brake. How did other men balance work pressures, the drive for success, and the desire to be a family man?

In spite of the small numbers, Jim, Pat, and I decided to continue to meet. As we talked that first week, we realized that we were all asking similar questions. We sensed how much we needed the friendship of other men. And so, for many weeks, we met like clockwork at seven on Friday mornings.

Pastor Jim was a short, friendly man whose graying beard and portly appearance made him immensely approachable. For most of the week, he wore blue jeans and faded tennis shoes. Entering his office, I noticed a few carefully selected books piled on his desk and his well-worn garage-sale couch. His office décor reflected his attitude that artificial appearance was too much of a burden to carry. He was always on the lookout for ways to simplify his life.

When I approached Pastor Jim about the possibility of forming a men's group, he was immediately interested. He offered that being a pastor had its own share of challenges, and he needed a place to "unload" at least as much as others do. "Pastors," he said, "can get too caught up in looking like they have it all together. The congregation doesn't want to hear that we can get overwhelmed at times. They don't want to think about us ever getting depressed. Heaven forbid that we would ever need to go for counseling."

Pat shared how being the controller of a small construction company was challenging. He talked about his feelings. "I know what it feels like for others to expect that I should have it all together. I try not to share my baggage with anyone. I'm never sure anyone really wants to hear how overwhelmed I feel at times. I work long hours and have a huge amount of responsibility at the job."

I could relate. "Being a psychologist is tough," I said. "People think that we should be able to handle anything that comes our way. We are never supposed to have marriage problems, get depressed, or struggle in our relationships. After all, we have all the answers."

"No, you don't," Jim chided. "We pastors really have all the answers. After all, we know the Bible, so we're never supposed to struggle with anything. Just trust and obey God, and everything will turn out fine."

And so we quickly established trust. We agreed to meet weekly and share our difficulties. I appreciated the opportunity to be vulnerable and transparent with these men I had known for some time. I found myself wanting more men to share this wonderful experience.

Our small group had a promising start. But later, reality came crashing in. The men I hoped would join began to attend, but they brough changes for which I was not prepared.

Several newcomers anxiously investigated the group. They came with at least as many questions as I had when I showed up for that first meeting. I had invited them to participate in a men's group, but they had no idea what to expect or how to behave. The veterans in the group shared their vision:

- to be consistent in attendance
- to keep one another's confidence
- to be vulnerable with one another
- to offer advice sparingly
- to pray for each other through the week

In spite of these clear directives and a supportive atmosphere, things quickly fell apart. I watched with deep regret as the integrity and purpose of the group began to erode.

- Attendance became sporadic.
- Men sometimes betrayed each other's confidences.
- They were often defensive and cautious.
- Their sharing was superficial.
- They offered easy answers in a dogmatic way.

I quickly became annoyed, though I was unsure of what to do with my irritation. For several weeks I simply watched the men dance around any substantial issues. They preferred to talk about the latest football game rather than discuss their relational difficulties. When serious topics came up, someone inevitably interrupted and lightened the tone. Joking was far easier than crying. I tried to model vulnerability by sharing pieces of my personal struggles. That seemed to have little impact. I asked questions that I hoped would take the men to a deeper place,

but no luck. They were obviously in pain, but they seemed incapable of going to their deeper, darker places. They expressed a
desire to explore inner feelings, but that territory was evidently
forbidden.

I watched the men come and go. I listened to what they said
and to the deeper message of what they meant. They repeatedly said that they were "fine," but their worlds were obviously
falling apart. I watched them grimace with the pain of being
rejected by a spouse but then say they could handle things. I
watched men lose jobs—their very livelihood—and fear for
their financial well-being but vow to land on their feet. Their
message was clear: Show no pain.

The good news was that the group did continue to meet,
albeit with a discernable limp. We could never seem to build
up enough steam to become a truly viable operation, but then,
I suppose that is a matter of perspective. I had envisioned a
group of six to ten members, hoping to create an environment
of safety where men could share their darkest secrets. We never
had a large group, but we did maintain four or five active members. Those that came seemed to appreciate the experience,
though they rarely shared their hidden darkness.

Men's Hidden Pain

The men's group lasted six years. Even though it never
became the safe haven for which I had hoped, I found myself
somewhat dependent on those weekly meetings. I wanted so
much to lay my issues on the table without hesitation and have
the others do the same. That rarely happened. These men were
simply too frightened to lift the lid of Pandora's box, wondering
what might possibly emerge and whether their "stuff" could

ever fit back in the box again. They were much more comfortable sharing their joys and triumphs than their sorrows and failures. They were comfortable being stuffed and hollow men.

Perhaps our men's group struggled under the weight of the unspoken code among men: *Do not share feelings of vulnerability.* For so long we have learned to hide our feelings, to never blush, to never show signs of weakness. When researchers Hammen and Peters studied many college roommates, they discovered that when women shared symptoms of depression with their friends, they found sympathy and caring. In contrast, when men shared similar feelings with their friends, they experienced social isolation and often outright hostility. These results have now been replicated by many other studies.[1]

Did our men's group have an impact on those who attended? Yes, to be sure. Did it reach men where they truly live? I don't think so.

After thinking for some time about the reasons for this, I have reached the following conclusions:

First, *men are uncomfortable sharing their inner pain.* By all indications, men have always been that way, and they don't show any indication of changing in the near future. Men do not want to walk into the abyss of sad, discouraging, depressive thoughts and feelings. They have found that if they ignore this seething cauldron, they can make it disappear. Of course this is never true, but most men continue to believe it.

Second, *men do not know how to put their feelings into words.* Early in life, boys are rarely taught how to share feelings. Instead their parents and teachers tell them, "Big boys don't cry." The boy who cries is often shamed, and he learns never again to be vulnerable. As an adult, he is reminded to keep a stiff upper lip.

Men have never had role models for talking about feelings. Such talk is a foreign language to us, and most of us prefer not to learn it. As men look around, they see other men who have learned not to cry or share vulnerable feelings. While many joke about men's inability to be sensitive, the message remains clear—most men are not about to become sensitive and transparent. Men have no language available for talking about depression.

Third, *men have no environment in which to share these vulnerable feelings.* We have men's golf clubs, fitness clubs, and perhaps even an occasional men's Bible study, but we have painfully few men's support groups. These safe containers for our shadowy feelings are rare indeed. And even when such havens are available, men are often unprepared to take advantage of them.

Since the breakup of the men's group at the church, I have been looking for a men's support group. However, I have nearly abandoned my search because I fear that such a group simply does not exist in my community. Such groups are few and far between, leaving the average man without any supportive places where he might explore painful experiences and emotions. This absence of support groups is a liability I live with when trying to help the men who do come for counseling.

Fourth, *our culture reinforces the exact opposite of sensitivity to painful feelings, inner explorations, and depressive symptoms.* Our culture loudly challenges men to be aggressive and demanding conquerors of challenges. The more a man can earn and the higher he rises on the ladder of success, the more recognition he obtains. He does not find admiration from his peers by seeking a men's support group. He finds their admiration by working a lot of hours, by having an impressive stock portfolio, by generating a large income, and by earning higher education degrees.

A man is far more likely to find relief and acceptance in a bar than a support group. The man who searches for an environment to talk about his profound discouragement is on a lonely quest indeed.

Finally, *the women in men's lives do not know how to encourage men to become acquainted with their feelings, losses, hopes, and dreams.* In many cases, instead of providing a nurturing environment, a man's family can actually pull him from his core being. Women are often attracted to "bad boys" who know how to live hard and play hard. The men who adorn the covers of popular magazines are rarely wholesome, sensitive, or spiritually directed. Women may say they want a man with sensitivity. However, I contend that they don't know what to look for in a man or how to help a man become more vulnerable.

A Pervasive Problem

Male depression is a silent and widespread epidemic. It is a classic example of a big, stinky elephant in the living room that no one knows how (or wants) to name, let alone tame. It is not only a stinky elephant but a lame one as well. Sometimes men's pain results in screams of agony, but most of the time it is just always there like a nagging toothache.

This sure and hidden darkness of male depression is largely an untreated phenomenon. Let's consider a few facts about male depression to put matters in perspective.

- The National Institute of Mental Health estimates that 6 to 10 percent of our population is struggling with depression. This is probably an underestimate because people are usually unwilling to admit that they are having problems.

- The symptoms of male depression are different from the symptoms women demonstrate.

- Women tend to internalize their pain, but men tend to externalize theirs, often in some form of acting out—alcoholism, marital problems, or struggles at work.

- Men rarely seek professional attention for their depression.

- Men tend to deny that anything is wrong.

- Professionals tend to overdiagnose depression in women and underdiagnose it in men.

Male depression is a malady with devastating consequences. Consider these statistics offered by Jed Diamond in his book *Male Menopause.*[2]

- Eighty percent of all suicides in the U.S. are by men.

- The suicide rate at midlife is three times higher for men than for women. At age 65, it is seven times higher.

- Sixty to eighty percent of depressed adults never get professional help. The statistics for men are unclear because of the hidden nature of depression.

- Eighty to ninety percent of people who seek help get relief from their symptoms.

- Four times as many men as women die by suicide even though women make more attempts.

Symptoms of Male Depression

Men struggle in a lonely world, but they are not alone. They are usually in a relationship—and that is where women come in. To understand your man and recognize the problems he is having, start by acquainting yourself with the symptoms of male depression. Learn how his depression is different from depression in women. Then, together, we can explore how to help him. Male depression differs significantly from female depression. In *Unmasking Male Depression*, Archibald Hart summarizes the symptoms of male depression.

• Irritability and hostility: Does your man overreact to small issues?

• Acting out, aggressiveness: Does he become verbally abusive at times?

• Low impulse control: Does he act without thinking?

• Displays anger when hurt: Does he react angrily when really hurt?

• Tendency to blame others and be unforgiving: Does he avoid accepting responsibility for his wrongdoing?

• Needs to maintain control: Is he overly controlling, and irritable if he feels out of control?

• Terrified to confront perceived weakness: Does he deny his weaknesses or limits?

• Higher willingness to take risks: Does he seem to enjoy high-risk activities?

• Behavior on the verge of social or legal standards: Does he bend the rules to fit his situation?

• Substance abuse and addictive behaviors (alcohol, nicotine): Does he indulge in substances or activities (such as exercise or gambling) excessively?

• General dissatisfaction with himself and his behavior: Is he generally unhappy and critical?

- Shame about depression: Is he reluctant to talk about depression or embarrassed to admit how he feels?[3]

Perhaps as you read this list you are nodding your head. These may be red flags that something is wrong. *Yes, my husband has some of these symptoms. Although he denies it, could he be depressed?* You realize his anger is not just anger. His blaming tendencies are not simply avoidance of accountability. His evening cocktails are not normal alcohol use—the picture is more complicated than that. His feelings of stress and irritability suggest something far more ominous—male depression.

Stephen came to see me after being referred by his employee assistance program at the local mill. He had been suspended with pay until I completed an assessment.

Stephen was a stocky man, about 30 years old, and perhaps 40 pounds overweight. His bushy beard and stern demeanor made him appear a bit menacing. He made sure I knew that he would never have come to a "shrink" had his employer not required him to.

"So why are you here, Stephen? What do you understand the reason to be for the referral?"

I already knew that he had been disciplined several times for taunting another worker and also for a physical altercation with another. The employee assistance worker wondered if alcohol abuse was part of the problem, but Stephen had no violations to date. The employee assistance worker wanted me to assess Stephen and see when he might be fit to return to work.

"To be honest, Doc," Stephen said coldly, "I think this is a bunch of bull. There's this guy at work who likes to dish it out but can't take it. When I give it back he goes running to the mill manager and cries for help. It's a pretty cowardly thing to do if you ask me."

Stephen stared at me, daring me to challenge his position. "What did this guy do to you, Stephen?"

"It's just a bunch of little stuff. He doesn't pull his weight at work. We all have to pick up the slack for his laziness. When we pick on him, he runs whining to the boss."

"But I didn't hear you say what he did to you," I said. "What made you so angry with him?"

"You'd have to be there, Doc. It's just mill mentality. He's a wuss. We challenge him to pick up the pace and he melts. None of us want him down there anymore."

"Sounds like you have this guy in your sights—you're going to pick on him until he leaves. Is that about it?"

"Yeah, I guess so. He needs to toughen up."

"What's this I hear about a physical altercation at work as well?"

"That's a bunch of bull, too. This guy talked trash about me behind my back. Nobody is going to do that and get away with it. That's probably not the way you would do it in your world, but it's the way it works in mine, and I'm not sorry for it one bit."

Over the next three weeks, Stephen and I continued to talk about the incidents. Although he showed little remorse for his actions, he reluctantly agreed to be careful about getting into these predicaments in the future. I reported this agreement, and his manager allowed him to return to work. More importantly, however, Stephen agreed to continue seeing me over the next several months. We explored his history of violence. He told a story similar to one I have heard many times before. He'd been raised by an angry, abusive father until he was ten. His parents divorced, and he only saw his father occasionally after that. Stephen carried a great deal of pain as a result of feeling rejected and abandoned. He felt that if he had been stronger his dad would not have left.

With that heritage, Stephen did not make the best husband, and his wife of 15 years had left him the year before because he had been demanding and abusive, replaying the very trait he hated in his father. Stephen seemed stoical about this loss, but clearly he hurt deeply about the divorce and being unable to see his children very often. He was dating another woman but stated clearly that he had no intention of letting anyone hurt him the way his ex-wife had. He was a man who had so much hidden pain—pain that could only be dealt with by building a wall between himself and his current girlfriend, by treating others harshly at work, and perhaps by abusing alcohol. His upbringing had effectively created a barrier between himself and the help he desperately needed.

From the Outside Looking In

So how does a woman feel as she watches her man self-destruct? How does she feel when she intuitively knows that something is terribly wrong, but all of her efforts to label the problem or find a remedy are rebuffed? I can only imagine how terrible and helpless she feels. I wonder if you struggle with these feelings:

- *Powerlessness.* You wish that you could help him label the problem. You wish that you could help him overcome his difficulties and find his elusive happiness.

- *Helplessness.* Always the fixer, you wish that you could reach into his hollow core and help him find a way out. You so desperately want him to be happy and whole.

- *Frustration.* At times you want to fix things for him because he won't do it for himself. You think you see clearly what needs to be done and want him to simply let you help him out of the mess that he is in.

- *Denial.* At times even you get caught up in denial. Because he so adamantly opposes your suggestions, you wonder if you are making too much of the problem.

- *Embarrassment.* You are embarrassed by his childish outbursts, his excessive drinking, and his social isolation. If he will not fix the problem and you cannot rescue him from his own pain, you are tempted to cover up the problem.

Your situation is a difficult one, but you can do some things to help. Your job is not to fix him. You do not have to rescue him or give up in despair. We will examine the symptoms of male depression, discuss how you can help, and consider the limits of your role. You will learn how to empower and encourage him to become healthy, but the choice will ultimately be his.

Women Can Help

What is it like to be a woman in a world where men act so much like...well, like men? A world where they are generally unfeeling, insensitive, domineering, and lacking social graces? A world where they create an impression that they are doing well even when their lives may be out of control?

As a woman, you feel it, you see it—you can almost touch it.

I know what it is like to live in a world where I, like other men, fumble around trying to meet the needs and desires of women. I know what it is like to be uncomfortable in my own skin, wishing I could put down many of the traits long associated with masculinity. The striving, driving, conquering impulses often seem like so much extra heavy armor, and the simple vulnerability of femininity appears so much lighter. But I am a man and will offer my impressions from that perspective.

I am also a psychologist and have worked with men and women for many years. I have witnessed the futile, destructive games that people play. Women are aware of our pain. Women have been created by the Master Designer with the ability to recognize our pain and the pain of our children. You know about it because you are sensitive, and you will set everything aside to tend your home and family. You are able to see things we would prefer to leave hidden in the silent, deadly reaches of our hearts. Uncertain, perhaps, of what to do about that dark and hidden pain, you still long to help. Please know that you can help us. This book will show you how.

You are likely reading this book because a man in your life may have the blues. You have found that his moodiness creates discomfort for you and your family. You know he carries heavy, hidden issues in the unspoken reaches of his life. You do not have to help, but you have the opportunity to help. You are in the uniquely powerful position of having a profound influence in his life.

This book is about how you can help your man find healing. Each chapter will focus on a different aspect of men's depression and on your role in the healing process. You may not feel powerful. In fact, you may feel that your efforts are in vain. You may believe that he is determined to be miserable in spite of your good intentions. That is not true. In most cases, he simply does not know how to receive your help, or you aren't sure how you can help. Keep reading, and don't give up hope!

A Helpmate

God, in His infinite wisdom, knew that man could wreck his life with very little effort. God must have smiled after He created man, pondering this brash, bold, swaggering creation.

Let me offer a "behind the scenes commentary" on the creation account. This is of course my own rendition of what might have happened, not to be confused with the reality of the text.

The Genesis story says that God created man from the dust of the ground. God's intention was for man to rule over creation, and so he did. Of all the creatures, man was and still is the only one capable of reason. We have the ability to use our brawn as well as our brains to accomplish what we set out to do. I wonder if, from this point on, man had a slight but perceptible foolhardiness. I wonder if we have taken God's prescription to manage creation and overdosed on it.

And so, in my version of creation, God saw that man would dare beyond reason, would conquer needlessly, would dominate unnecessarily.

Perhaps God also saw that man's reasoning abilities were limited. Could he be counted on to manage something as grand as the universe? Perhaps, God thought, the wise thing to do would be to balance out this aspect of creation with something a bit more reflective, sensitive, caring. And so He announced that it was not good for man to be alone, or on his own, or left to his own mischievous devices. God's solution has been applauded since the dawn of creation—woman!

Did God design a helpmate to balance out man's desperate difficulty in managing his moods? Did God know that man would be so utterly outward directed that he would have little ability to know his own heart and the brooding darkness hidden there? We have no evidence of such reasoning, but I believe that God knew then what we most certainly know now: Men tend to hide their pain and often need help to know the longings hidden inside.

A Few Ways for Women to Help

First, *learn to recognize and be informed about male depression.* You can do little to help your man deal with his depression if you do not know the symptoms. Acquaint yourself with the disguised aspects of male depression and the difference between male and female depression. (We will discuss that in the following chapter.)

Second, *find ways to help your man talk about his distress.* This means that you would do well not to challenge him on the issue or shame him in any way. Rather, let him know that you know something is wrong and you want to help him find solutions to his problems. Help him understand that you are an ally; you know that he does not feel good, and you want to help him feel better.

Third, *if he is constantly defensive, which is quite possible, you may need to be mildly confrontational.* You may need to consistently and calmly tell him that the problem will not simply disappear on its own.

His depression is likely to express itself in many ways. It may appear as alcohol abuse, a disquieting anger, or distance in your relationship. Whatever form it takes, maintain your conviction that ignoring the problem will not make it disappear.

No Way to Live

Living in a home with a depressed man can be challenging. You may feel as if you are walking on eggshells, wondering when one will break. This is no way to live, and thankfully, you do not have to keep living this way. You can help your man find answers for his blues and emerge from his hidden darkness.

By recognizing how you may be enabling his sulking, brooding blues, you will be better equipped to confront such destructive behavior. As we move through the book together, we will explore many different ways you can help your man move beyond depression.

But We Handle Things So Differently! Depression in Women and Men

The mass of men live lives of quiet desperation.

—Henry David Thoreau

Between appointments I glanced at the messages stacked in my box. I had tried to ignore them for the first few hours of the day, hoping some might magically disappear if I paid them no mind. None cooperated. By mid morning the pile had grown too large for me to ignore.

I grabbed the pile and took the messages back to my desk. There they would sit until afternoon when I finally fought off my procrastination and began sifting through them.

The first message was from a client, letting me know that she could not attend a group session that evening due to illness. No problem. We would simply reschedule. The next was from a student at a local college who was looking for a guest speaker for her psychology class. I put that one off until I had time to examine my calendar.

The next note said that Peggy J. had called last night and left a message with my after-hours answering service. "Peggy J. says she used to be your client about ten years ago. Her husband is depressed and says he doesn't love her anymore. He says he's in love with a woman they work with. She is crying a lot, having trouble sleeping, and needs to see you right away. Please call."

I hadn't heard from Peggy in years. I tried to recall the circumstances of her visits so long ago. I remembered her as a fiery woman and a hard worker who must have been about 45 at that time, which would make her nearly 55 now. I recalled her husband, Jerry, as being a constant source of difficulty for her. He struggled with depression but was unwilling to get treatment for it. They had come in for several sessions but had broken off contact prematurely because Jerry was not interested in professional help.

I suppose I shouldn't have been surprised to hear that things had not gotten better, but I was sad to learn that Peggy was doing poorly. She was struggling with symptoms that many people experience during a crisis—including sleeplessness and emotional overload—but her dilemma was much greater. The note indicated that her husband was in love with another woman and that their marriage was in jeopardy. I wondered about Jerry's depression and whether this was another indirect expression of his inner turmoil. Was he still struggling with untreated depression? Would he now be willing to come in for counseling? Was he considering giving up on their marriage? I feared that he would react as most men do—by hiding his pain.

I paused for a moment and said a short prayer. "Lord, You know what Peggy needs right now. You know her situation. You know what Jerry needs. Please give me the strength and wisdom to know what to say to her."

When I dialed Peggy's number, she answered the phone on the first ring. She sounded drawn and discouraged. There was little of the fire that I remembered. After a brief exchange of pleasantries, Peggy plunged into an explanation of her dilemma.

"Jerry just told me that he's in love with a woman we work with. To make things even worse, she's a good friend of ours. He says that he can't help his feelings."

"How long has this been going on?" I asked.

"That's the crazy thing. He just announced this two days ago. He says he has not had any kind of physical relationship with her, but still, he says he loves her. I have talked to her, and she says she loves him too—like a brother. She says she is not interested in romance and won't get in the middle of our relationship. The whole thing is crazy."

"So, Peggy," I said slowly, "he's never spent time alone with this woman? They have no real love relationship?"

"I can't see how he could really love her. He doesn't truly know her. As far as I know they have never slept together. This is just some weird infatuation thing with him. I don't know how else to explain it."

"Tell me about your relationship with Jerry. How have things been with you two?"

"That is another crazy thing. I thought things had been fine. We're both getting ready to retire. We just bought a motor home, and we've been looking at some property in Arizona. We've had a lot of fun times this year, and planning our retirement has been great. I thought we were best friends. But to hear him tell it, things have been lousy. He has hurt me deeply, but

I have to admit that I'm also scared to death that he's going to leave me."

"What has Jerry said about your relationship?"

"He told me that he hasn't been in love with me for years. In fact, he says he's been thinking about leaving me for ten years. He says he wants to be with her. I just can't believe it."

Peggy cleared her throat. She was obviously crying. When she apologized for her tears, I caught a glimpse of the tough woman I had counseled years before.

"You're certainly entitled to feel bad about what is happening, Peggy. No apologies necessary. Give yourself permission to hurt. This is a huge crisis. Let me look at my schedule. I'll get you in as soon as possible."

"Thank you, Dr. Hawkins. I need some help before I lose it completely."

My secretary buzzed me. "Your next appointment is here." I had another client waiting for me, but I was having trouble escaping the sadness of the moment. In the past two weeks, I'd heard from three women whose husbands were in the process of leaving them, either physically or emotionally. In fact, I had received many calls similar to Peggy's in the past few months. In some cases, women were abandoning men, but most often I was hearing from wives whose husbands wanted out of the marriage. What was happening?

Anatomy of a Crisis

Peggy was able to get an appointment early the next week. When she entered the waiting room of my office, I barely recognized her. She looked much older than her years. She had the gaunt look of one who has lost too much weight too quickly. Her cheeks were sunken into her face, and her skin was wrinkled and worn. Her graying hair was stringy and unkempt. She wore blue jeans and work boots, reminding me of the hard-working woman I had known her to be. She forced a smile when she saw me.

I escorted Peggy into my office. She offered a few ice-breakers, but I quickly steered the conversation to her relationship with Jerry.

"So, how are you, really, Peggy?"

"How do I look?" she said, gesturing to her face and the wrinkles around her eyes. "You don't have to tell me. I know I look like heck. I've lost nearly eight pounds in the past two weeks. I wanted to lose weight, but this is a rough way to do it. I feel horrible, and I can't seem to keep anything down."

"Let's try to figure out what is going on and what you can do about it."

I met with Peggy regularly over the next few months, helping her sort out what was happening. I saw her alone because Jerry steadfastly refused to come in for counseling. Together, Peggy and I pieced together the puzzle of her life. It was similar to one with which I am well acquainted, one with many of the mysterious pieces having to do with the peculiar behavior of men.

We can assess Jerry's situation from many different perspectives, but let's consider the possibility that his actions represent an aspect of male depression. As Peggy and I talked about her current crisis, we clearly saw that Jerry was not truly in love with their friend—at least not in the way that most of us define love. Rather, he was in love with *his fantasy* of their friend. He had idealized her in his mind. Apparently, they had never come close to consummating their "affair." Peggy believed they had never even been alone, except for perhaps a few minutes here and there at work. Jerry told Peggy that he admired their friend and wanted to be with someone who was funny and lively and who liked him. This was mind-boggling to Peggy because she believed she possessed those very qualities.

Even though their mutual friend clearly stated that she had no interest in having a relationship with Jerry, he continued to cling to his fantasy.

Peggy shared the history of their 25-year marriage, some of which I had heard during our previous sessions. She insisted that she had been happy with Jerry, but she did not believe he had ever overcome his depression. The history of Jerry's depression provides a chronicle of the all too common failure of men to express their emotions in healthy ways. The following signs fit the pattern precisely:

- refusing to communicate
- withdrawing into silence
- hiding behind hobbies
- gradually losing friendships
- becoming increasingly sullen and tired
- becoming increasingly irritable and angry

As I listened to Peggy tell the story of her failed attempts to get Jerry to talk with her or to get him into counseling, I assured her that this current crisis, in all likelihood, had little to do with her. Rather, it was a series of his disguised attempts to deal with the inner pain of male depression. I helped her understand what was happening and why men tended to do exactly as Jerry had been doing—hiding and denying his pain.

Depressive Confusion

Peggy and I explored Jerry's depression vicariously, without the benefit of him being there.

"He says that he doesn't have a problem," Peggy said. "He admits that he has been depressed in the past, but he insists that he is doing fine now. According to him, I'm the one who is depressed. And to some degree, I suppose he's right. I am more depressed now than ever. I'm the one taking antidepressants."

"Don't allow what he says to confuse you," I said. "What men tell us and what is actually happening are often very different stories."

Les Carter and Frank Minirth, in their book *The Freedom from Depression Workbook,* give us a working definition of depression. It is an extremely helpful guide to understanding depressive symptoms.

> A good working definition of depression would be a feeling of sadness and dejection resulting in an increasingly pessimistic outlook on life. Included in depression can be a mental dullness as demonstrated by poor concentration and a breakdown in reasoning abilities. It is usually accompanied by such symptoms as social withdrawal, decreased motivation, lessened sex drive (or conversely a willingness toward normally unthinkable immorality), sleep disturbances, increased anxiety, edginess, and critical thoughts.[1]

This summary is both comprehensive and accurate. It is also consistent with many other volumes on depression and an excellent guide for people struggling with the debilitating effects of the blues. If you have ever struggled with depression, you will likely see yourself in these words. Unfortunately, however, the list stops short of explaining how male depression differs from female depression. This is where I was able to help Peggy understand Jerry and to give her a few more options for her own life.

Confusion about male depression abounds. As far as I know, the book you have in your hands is the only one of its kind designed to help women understand how their husbands experience depression. Undoubtedly, you will be relieved to know that you are not crazy. The signs you have observed in your husband are probably evident in the majority of men who suffer from depression. He acts so different from the way he did when he was happy. He seems depressed, yet he doggedly denies being depressed. In fact, he angrily tells you to back off and leave him alone. What is going on?

Differences in Symptoms of Depression

As I have suggested, most books on depression have been written mostly for and about women. Many experts are finally beginning to see that male depression has received far too little attention. Why? This deficit has several possible explanations.

- Women are more open with their feelings of depression.
- Women seek help more frequently than men do.
- Most studies explore women's depression to a greater degree than men's.

Most current researchers believe that male depression is underdiagnosed because of secrecy and shame. Dr. Archibald Hart, Professor of Psychology and former dean of the Graduate School of Psychology at Fuller Theological Seminary, is the author of *Unmasking Male Depression*. He notes some of the significant differences between male and female depression. He says, "Angry outbursts, becoming easily annoyed, increased sexual activity, workaholism, emotional and social withdrawal, coldness, aloofness, and even forms of family violence are nearer the depression mark than the crying and hopelessness of female depression."[2] Perhaps some of the following descriptions will sound familiar to you.

Blame

Hart says that women tend to blame themselves. Women are generally willing to accept responsibility for problems in themselves and their families. By contrast, men tend to blame others. They use rationalizations, excuses, and other defenses to avoid accepting responsibility for their actions.

I can see some of you grinning already as you read this. "Yup," you say. "I can never get my husband to admit to anything, even if he is caught in the act. He will make excuses and then get furious if I make him own up to problems. The more I press him, the more defensive he gets."

Having been a participant and leader in men's groups for years, I would say that Hart has hit the nail on the head. Men are loath to admit problems because doing so makes us feel more inadequate. Let's consider some other differences between the ways men and women deal with depression.

Sadness

In my counseling experience, women tend to express the classic symptoms of depression, including sadness, apathy, and worthlessness. Women are willing to feel their vulnerabilities

while men—are you ready?—tend to project the problem outward.

Men tend to feel anger much more easily than sadness. They
don't want to feel sadness, perhaps because of what society in
general and fathers in particular have taught them: Men don't
feel sad—they get mad, and then they get even.

My experience with men and their feelings is rather discouraging. I have joked before about using a chart with men to
teach them to accurately identify their feelings. "This is sadness,"
I say, referring to the little face with the downward turned mouth.
"This is contentment," I continue, pointing to a calm face with
lips turned slightly upward. However, even with these visual cues,
men seem to resist attempts to identify their feelings.

Lest I sound like I am being overly critical of men, I believe
that they come by these problems honestly. Ronald Levant
agrees in his book and videotape series titled *Men and Emotions.*

> A bedrock issue is the difficulty men have in identi-
> fying—indeed, in differentiating—their emotional
> states. In addition to its negative impact on the psy-
> chological well-being, physical health, and interper-
> sonal relationships, this deficit presents a serious
> impediment to therapy for deeper issues.... To be good
> men, they were told, they must become reliable pro-
> viders, emotionally stoic, logical, solution-oriented, and
> aggressive.[3]

Anxiety and Fear

Feeling sad is not the only emotional challenge for men.
They have trouble with many other emotions as well, including
anxiety and fear. Women tend not only to feel these emotions

but also to share them with others. They are not ashamed to say they have a tendency to be nervous about things.

Women also tend to look to men to protect them from the big bad world. This certainly is a cultural phenomenon, perhaps reinforced by biological factors. Rather than feel frightened or admit to those feelings, men tend to feel suspicious and guarded. They have a very difficult time trusting others. Because of this distrust, they would be likely to avoid disclosing their feelings even if they could learn to identify them.

In my men's group, trust seemed to be a huge issue. Our members were willing to share only a limited amount of information, and we could never really talk about why this was so. Maybe we didn't want anyone to think we were too weak to solve our own problems. Perhaps we feared other men talking badly about us behind our backs. Whatever the reasons, the group had an unspoken rule: Don't share—it's not safe.

Because of distrust, men tend to be isolated from other people. This isolation begins early in life. In their seminal book on boys, *Real Boys Workbook,* William Pollack and Kathleen Cushman state that boys tend to develop a vicious circle of loneliness. They assert that boys learn early to be fearful of showing any feelings of vulnerability. Hiding behind a mask, they believe that no one understands them and slip into feelings of despair.[4]

Creating Conflict

This issue is huge. Relationships cannot survive with too much conflict, and men—bless their hearts—tend to create more conflict than they resolve. This is certainly a generalization, but women tend to avoid conflict (or internalize it), and men tend to create conflict (by externalizing their distress). Dr.

Hart suggests that men tend to act out their inner turmoil, and women will turn their emotions inward—feeling them.

I discontinued counseling some time ago with a couple that epitomized this problem. Jennifer was a kind, sensitive, caring Christian woman, liked by all, whose feelings were hurt on nearly a daily basis by her abrupt and confrontational husband, Tad. He alleged, "I would rather tell her exactly what I think. I want her to know exactly where I stand on issues. If something bugs me, I'm going to let her know."

Tad felt free to share his candid, negative opinion about his wife's choice of clothing, even if she had taken great time and pleasure in picking out just the right outfit that might please him and her. He seemed to take no time to reflect when she told him that such comments were hurtful. He, of course, had a ready defense and explanation.

Tad had an extremely difficult time understanding why his bluntness was ruining their marriage. Even with repeated feedback from me and his wife, he defended his right to say things unvarnished, precisely the way he perceived them to be. I worked with Tad and Jennifer for nearly a year, primarily trying to help him share his feelings in a more compassionate and honest manner. I tried to help him empathize with her pain, and I encouraged her to stop internalizing conflict and share her feelings directly.

In the end, Jennifer chose to divorce Tad. She decided that she could not put up with his rude and coarse behavior. She was unwilling to let him deride her and call her names when he was angry. She could not tolerate his habit of constantly finding fault with her actions and bluntly telling her about them. She decided that she simply did not like his character—in particular, his tendency to create conflict.

Jennifer and Tad are similar to many couples. In numerous relationships, one person tends to be more "truthful," thus creating conflict. The other person leans toward being tactful and avoiding conflict. This kind of equation generally does not work in marriage. Both partners need to learn to deal with their inevitable unhappiness in an honest but conciliatory manner.

Nice or Hostile

Unfortunately, our culture trains women to be "nice." It shapes them to be subservient to men. Some churches have even twisted Scripture to reinforce this passive, demeaning role. On the other hand, our culture trains men to be overtly or covertly hostile and controlling. Some men have been quick to use Ephesians 5:22 (Wives, submit to your husbands as to the Lord) as a justification for this controlling attitude. Yet many wink at the previous verse (Submit to one another out of reverence for Christ) or the verses that follow that command a man to honor his wife as Christ loved the church—by giving himself up for her.

Consider the men that you have known. How many have an edge that at times was hard to understand? You sensed their anger and hostility, but when you confronted them about it, they denied it. Perhaps their covert hostility was a blind spot for them as well. Perhaps it was so ingrained that they weren't even aware of it. Regardless, you felt their hostility, and it was uncomfortable for you.

A man's friends can help him by confronting him about his hostility and holding him accountable for it. Recently, a man scheduled a counseling appointment with me. Because men rarely volunteer to attend therapy, I suspected that Dennis was there by compulsion either because of a problem with hostility or because his family had already left and he was trying to pick up the pieces.

After Dennis sank into the chair, I could tell that he was very distressed. His eyes were sunk deep into his head. His face was expressionless as he told of his wife and son leaving him. He was discouraged because this was his fourth marriage and he really wanted this one to work. But, he said softly, "They think I'm an angry, hostile man."

His wife had taken the only reasonable path available to her. She told him, in front of their pastor, that either he needed to work on his hostility—and the accompanying depression—or she would not allow him back in their home. Her approach was effective. Dennis is coming in for treatment on a regular basis. His wife is no longer content to play the prescribed role as "the nice one." She has taken a stand that combines love and an insistence that Dennis commit to change.

Attack or Withdraw When Hurt

Men and women deal with hurt in entirely different ways. According to Dr. Hart, women tend to withdraw when they are hurt. A woman may wait for months before telling a man about what he did to hurt her feelings. Men rarely understand the pain they are causing, in part because they tend to deny it.

Men, on the other hand, are inclined to attack when they are hurt. They often cannot or will not label their pain as "hurt," but they will let you know that they are upset. They tend to transform various feelings into anger, and hurt is certainly one of those feelings. When under duress, men tend to go on the offensive.

A woman can help her man to recognize his hurt, much as she might do with a young child. Of course, she would do well not to patronize him or make him feel like a child. Rather, she can simply say, "I didn't intend to hurt your feelings. I am sorry." These simple words often go a long way toward diffusing his anger.

Boundaries

Boundaries seem to be barometers for how life is going. Watch how people handle their personal boundaries, and you will learn a lot about them.

Most women have trouble setting personal boundaries. If they assert themselves and say no, they often feel guilty. If they want something from someone, they often have difficulty asking for it.

Men also have trouble with boundaries and control, though their problem is a bit more obtuse. They are likely to be over-controlling because they fear being out of control. They often set rigid boundaries to protect themselves. A man in my men's group made a comment recently that illustrates this rigidity in boundaries. He said that he didn't trust women and would not allow any to get too close to him. What he didn't realize was that he actually didn't trust himself. He didn't trust that he could set healthy limits, allowing the right kinds of women close while steering clear of others. He thought in terms of extremes and black-or-white thinking and could not live with the vagueness of "gray" challenges.

Men who are depressed may have even more trouble with boundaries. You may notice your man becomes incredibly rigid when he tells you what he will and won't do. He may "take a stand" when such rigidity is actually unnecessary. He may feel as if you are attacking his boundaries when you are simply trying to negotiate. He is telling you, indirectly, that he does not fully trust himself or others.

Again, gentle assurance that you understand his needs and will not violate his boundaries, assuming they are realistic, will go a long way toward easing his mind. You can gently point out to him his black-or-white position, showing him that many other possibilities exist. "Is it possible…" is often a nice way to approach these kinds of issues. Also, he will need to do some work within himself so that he does not feel so fragile and vulnerable.

Talking About Weakness

Women typically enjoy gathering with other women to talk about their lives. They have learned the fine art of sharing with one another, offering support, and giving advice. Women are gatherers, and they tend to gather together.

Well, you guessed it. Men do not want to share their hurts openly. That would be a definite sign of weakness, and men have been trained not to show their soft underbellies. Men who struggle with the blues have an even greater tendency to hide their weaknesses. The dark clouds of depression make them feel weak. They feel even weaker if they consider seeking help.

My friend Stan is a family physician. He tells me that one of his greatest frustrations is that men are incredibly reluctant to seek medical help. They are likely to wait until they are on their deathbeds before coming in for assistance. Getting them to come in for their annual exams is nearly impossible, and rarely will they heed his advice to get rectal and prostate exams after age 50. He watches helplessly as they work too hard, sleep too little, and generally take poor care of their bodies. In many ways, they set themselves up for both physical sickness and depression.

Recently, a military officer and his wife came to me for counseling. Tim and Cathy had been having problems for years, but he had been unwilling to seek help until she told him she would

leave if he didn't attend counseling. Cathy had watched helplessly as Tim self-destructed. She watched him become more
and more isolated, withdrawn, and irritable. When I was finally
able to convince him to share his story, he revealed a great deal
about the problems he was having.

"I've been in the military for 15 years. We are told not to
fraternize with the enlisted men. That leaves a small percentage
of people that I can actually talk to. On top of that, my training
tells me that I should be able to handle anything that comes
my way. After all, if I can lead troops in combat, I should be
able to take care of my relationship with my wife, and I certainly should be able to handle my emotional life."

Tim bore a heavy burden. Cathy's burden was equally heavy.
They lived in a larger culture that does not encourage weakness and a smaller culture, the military, where self-reliance was
a central requirement of the job. We need to ask ourselves
whether we expect too much of men.

I shared with Tim and Cathy how coming to counseling was
a huge first step toward healing. Together we could analyze what
was not working and find practical solutions. We could bring
the problem out of the darkness and find answers. Over the
following weeks, we explored how their toughness created a
barrier between them. I shared that intimacy was ultimately
"into me see." They seemed to appreciate this instruction and
consented to be vulnerable with one another.

Top Dog vs. Blending In

Another burden carried by many men is the "alpha male"
syndrome. Men feel a strong need to be competitive and in
charge. They are reluctant to share their dark feelings because
they need to be in command of their situation. Like Tim, the

men feel as if they are in a military situation even when they are not. Letting another man take the "top" position, by providing psychological help, for example, is a real challenge for most men. Reaching out for nurturance or guidance from women is equally challenging for many men.

Women, on the other hand, are usually comfortable with blending in. In fact, they feel an innate need to belong. They feel far less compulsion to be competitive or to come out on top of others. Men try to maintain a strong male image, but women may disintegrate at the slightest failure. This is partially what makes women inclined to ask for help.

Self-Medication

Women feel distressed as often as do men. They often have their own maladies, including depression and low self-esteem. Women, however, are much more likely than men to seek counseling for their depression. Women also are inclined to develop destructive coping strategies that include using food, friends, and "love" to self-medicate. Becoming excessively codependent on friends, to the detriment of their own understanding and values, can be very damaging to their self-esteem.

Men use numerous destructive vices to cope with their discouragement:

- use alcohol excessively
- watch too much television
- engage too much in sports, either actively or vicariously
- demand too much sexual activity
- gamble too much
- work excessively

Do you hear your man use any of these rationalizations?

- A few beers help me unwind.
- It's just my way of blowing off some steam.
- I just need to zone out in front of the tube.
- It's not hurting anybody.
- I am just like every other man I know.

And the list could continue. He offers explanations for and defenses against any perceived criticism. He doesn't want anyone to challenge his lifestyle. Why? Because he needs these things and activities to self-medicate against inner pain. If you attack him for these weaknesses, you will awaken the sleeping giant, and it may not be pretty.

But what is "excessive" behavior? He says it is not too much, and you say it is. Who is right? As a general rule I suggest to couples that if something is a problem for one partner, it is a problem. Let me illustrate. If the wife feels that the husband is spending too much time on the river fishing with his buddies, their relationship has a problem. Likewise, if the husband feels that his wife is spending too much money buying clothes, they have a relational issue that they must address. *If something is a problem for one, it is a problem for both.* Don't be dissuaded from feeling uncomfortable about any particular issue.

Am I Lovable?

Both sexes struggle with doubts about feeling loved. Women tend to wonder if they are loveable enough. They question whether they have performed or conformed enough to meet the expectations of the man in their life. The question is different with men, however.

Men constantly wonder if they are being loved enough. They wonder if they are getting the love they deserve or if they are with the right woman—the one who can give them everything they are entitled to.

Over the past several years, I worked with many men who were truly challenged by this problem. They felt an intense emptiness inside that they hoped their spouse would fill. Failing to recognize that a major part of the issue had to do with their own insecurity, they sought relief from an external source. This is not an unusual occurrence in the field of psychology—many of us wish that something or someone outside our self could heal our wounds. We give away far too much power to someone who is destined to disappoint us. In a manner of speaking, we make an idol out of those we wish could do miraculous things for us. Men often learn the hard way that the relief they seek must come from their own hard work and by placing their trust in God alone.

A Definite Diagnosis

Recently, I have been battling a spate of colds that have disrupted my life. They are a nuisance to my general ability to function, and I have become impatient with them. At times, I also found myself wondering if my doctor had made an accurate diagnosis. "Be patient," he advised. "Colds just take time to run their course."

And so I attempt to practice patience, sniffling and snorting, taking cold medicine that sometimes makes the cure seem worse than the illness. But all the while I wonder if my doctor was right. Finally, in a fit of frustration, I call him again and tell him that something else must be going on. "We need to get to the bottom of things," I insist. Although I feel awkward about being so assertive, I strongly state, "I think this is more than a cold. I have all these symptoms, and they are not going away. Can we look a little deeper?" We do, and we find other problems that need attention. He makes a different diagnosis, a bacterial infection, offers some antibiotics, and—*voila!*—I am on the way to health.

That is what we are after as we consider all the ways that men and women handle their depression. If you hear yourself justifying his behavior…

- He's just a little moody.
- He's just going through a tough time.
- He can't help it because work has been hard on him.
- You can't expect any more out of him.

…then you will never make an accurate diagnosis, and you surely will never find a cure. This list of excuses will help you know what to be watching for so that you can understand the problem and determine possibilities for healing.

Much of the remainder of this book will address solutions. But now you know what men's depression looks like and how it differs from what women experience. This will be a powerful beginning that will lead to effective diagnosis and treatment.

Elijah Caving In

Men have had difficulty dealing with their emotions for a long time, and many cope by retreating into their personal caves. This drives many women crazy, yet men still withdraw.

Elijah is an interesting example of male depression. We read in 1 Kings of the battle between the forces of good and evil, an ancient skirmish between one prophet of God and nearly a thousand pagan priests. The odds certainly would not have been on Elijah's side, if not for the fact that he was delivering a message from the Lord.

Elijah's message was simple and blunt: "There will be neither dew nor rain in the next few years except at my word" (1 Kings 17:1). So much for a message to win friends and forge unity.

After delivering his message of doom and gloom, Elijah was, understandably, not a popular fellow. Over the next three years, he traveled from place to place and was often forced to remain in hiding. But he was repeatedly encouraged by witnessing the hand of the Lord—seeing the fire of the Lord burn up his offering before the people of Israel, triumphing over the four hundred prophets of the idol Baal, and being fed by ravens.

But our story of the victorious, wandering warrior takes a dramatic turn. When he is personally threatened by Queen Jezebel, Elijah runs like a frightened rabbit, losing himself in the desert. Eventually, he finds a cave to hole up in. But, as is the case with so many men today, the "cave" does not provide the refuge he had expected. Instead, it adds to his growing burden, resulting in even more discouragement and despair. Elijah's experience can teach us some lessons.

Elijah becomes very discouraged and finally cries out in a moment of depression: "I have had enough, Lord. Take my life. I am no better than my ancestors." There it is. A man of God asking to die. Why?

- *Exhaustion.* Elijah, like many men today, had failed to deal with years of pent-up emotions. His energies had been consumed by lack of sleep, poor diet, and inadequate leisure.

- *Fear.* Pursued to the point of constant exhaustion and fear, he had little emotional or spiritual energy to combat these troubling feelings.

- *Loneliness.* Elijah, like many men today, attempted to fight his battles alone and could not help but succumb to emotional exhaustion.

- *Futility.* With little encouragement and so many things going wrong, Elijah slipped into despair.

I wonder whether a woman might have handled Elijah's traumatic experience in a different manner. Without being facetious, I wonder if she might have called her friends, sought counsel, and enlisted support from caring people around her. I doubt that she would have isolated herself in a cave in the desert. But that is the point of this chapter—men handle their depression very differently than women do.

A Clearer Idea

Are men from Mars and women from Venus? I am not so sure about that, but they are certainly different, and we had best come to terms with those differences if we are to build and maintain healthy relationships.

After reviewing the factors related to male depression that I have described in this chapter, you probably have a clearer idea about whether your man has the blues. As we move together through this book, you will find more strategies for helping men who have symptoms of depression.

The Courage to Cry: Defensiveness and Denial

Every act of creation begins with an act of destruction.

—PICASSO

WORKING WITH MEN OCCUPIES A LARGE PART of my life as a psychologist. Actually, I sit on both sides of the couch when it comes to men's issues. I not only have participated in a men's group for years but also conduct a men's therapy group. I also occasionally attend personal sessions with a male counselor. Thus, I can speak with some authority about what makes men tick.

I have been a specialist in men's issues for years and have written two books on the topic. Part of my focus has included the issue of violence—a topic that, tragically, seems central to men. As I mentioned earlier in this book, men's emotions tend to come out in indirect and often hostile ways. We are notorious for drinking too much, acting too brashly, treating people too insensitively, and generally getting into trouble.

Violence is one powerful way in which men indirectly express feelings and cover up depression. Many people seem to believe domestic violence is limited to the act of men hitting women. Certainly it includes that, but you may also know that domestic violence extends far beyond pushing or hitting. It is about power and control, and it is far more pervasive in our society than many believe. Men often vow that they would never be violent with a woman. Those who do resort to violence try to rationalize it as justifiable. They moralize and pontificate about it during their early stages of counseling. Most espouse very narrow definitions of violence. They do not consider these activities abusive:

- controlling their spouses' spending
- monitoring their spouses' time
- criticizing their spouses' friends or family
- calling their spouses names when angry
- demanding that their spouses worship a certain way
- demanding that their spouses agree with them

My job in anger management and domestic violence treatment groups is to change their minds.

Most people think that men who attend mandated treatment are simply angry. They erroneously believe that these men's personalities and their accompanying problems can be explained by their anger. Although anger is the symptom, the root problem runs much deeper. I see men who have lost heart. I see men who have lost touch with the things that used to excite them. I see men who have sold their dreams and hopes and, in quiet desperation, have purchased a mundane lifestyle that has led to depression. These are the men that John Eldredge, author of *Wild at Heart*, would say have lost their spirit of adventure. They have moved so far from the things that excite them that all that remains is disguised malaise.

Working as a psychologist in a men's domestic violence treatment group is both professionally rewarding and intensely frustrating. Sometimes I think this group of men is very different from the general population. Most times, however, I think the vast majority of men are the same. Let me share a recent group experience that will give you a glimpse into the way that many men think.

Group Therapy

The men file into the group one by one, greeting each other with feigned joviality. Tension fills the air immediately—they have mixed feelings about being here. They seem to enjoy one another, but this is the last place they would choose to be on a Wednesday afternoon. But attendance is mandatory due to their legal sanctions. Most have to attend the group for a year and stay free from any other legal offenses.

Most men resent the cost and rarely pass up opportunities to make snide comments about it—"He's making a bundle off us tonight"—before moving on to light banter with one another. These men have elevated sarcasm to an art form. Passive aggression and other defenses are rigidly established qualities with most of them. If I attack these patterns too directly, the men could explode in anger—something I am not always prepared to handle.

I ask the men to follow some rules that will create respect within the group. I ask them to keep things confidential, to watch their language, to be prompt, to do their homework. This may be the only place where some of these men have been treated with respect. It is also one of the few places where they are required to treat others with respect.

The group has seven members ranging in age from 23 to 55. Five of them have been charged with domestic violence against their partners. One is there because of violence against another man, one as a result of violence against his own child. Their shame is hidden just below the surface, right beside their depression.

Though some would deny it, these men are "typical." Every man in the group is working, many of them too hard and too long. However, they do not see workaholism as a problem. "You do what you have to do," they say nonchalantly. Five are married, one is separated because of violence in the home, and two are divorced. Generally, they are rough, tough all-American men. Two attend church. All say they believe in God.

This group is conservative. They are hard-working, patriotic, and say they love their families. They believe in their right to own weapons and resent that these rights have been taken away because of their crimes.

They are not insightful. They struggle to see patterns in their thinking and their behavior. They struggle to get beneath the surface to examine what makes them tick. They cannot see that their behavior may reveal underlying depression. As with most men, they deny any suggestion that they are depressed, in spite of evidence to the contrary.

My task with these rough-and-tumble men is to gain their respect and then, hopefully, change their behavior. The courts have charged me with a huge responsibility. In the process of altering these men's thinking and actions, I would like to help them with their depression, for I believe that is a central cause of the problem of violence in the home.

I take any chance I get to point out that no one single incident landed them in this group. They each had repeated problems with power and control. I work hard to encourage them to take responsibility for their physically or emotionally abusive behavior.

On this particular evening, we dealt with the issue of sexual integrity. This is part of learning to treat others with respect and not take advantage of others in any way. I presented the material—the importance of mutual respect, trust, and honesty in a sexual relationship. I was not prepared for the rousing discussion that followed. The room was electric with energy as the newcomers showed off both their ignorance and their sexism, and the veterans blamed others and rationalized and minimized their offenses. Again, I listened and watched for symptoms of depression disguised in other forms. Herein lies the key to so many problems because if a man cannot care for himself, he cannot truly care for others.

"If a woman doesn't respect herself, I don't see why I should have to respect her," one man said. "She knows what she's getting into."

"Women don't want men to treat them nice. They like bad boys," another said, his eyes searching the room for approval.

"Yeah. Why is it all up to the man to provide the integrity? What about the responsibility of the woman?" a newcomer added.

"It's really not taking advantage of her if she's willing," one of the veterans said gruffly.

At this point, the men were looking at me defiantly. The newcomers waited to see how I would deal with their points of view. The veterans watched me, smiling, knowing that I had little tolerance for opinions that marginalized women. They knew that in a few moments I would firmly point out the error of their thinking. Outside of the group, they put women down, making derogatory comments, but not here. Outside of the group they joked about and demeaned women. "Might as well get them before they get you," one man had said. I would not tolerate those attitudes here, and I hoped to change the way they viewed and treated women.

I looked around the room. They came from backgrounds where moral values were in short supply. They had seen a side of the world that I had never experienced. Most had fathers who had taught their sons to be tough, to trust no one, to avoid wincing in the face of pain. Their histories included being humiliated for acting anything less than John Wayne. They were taught to be strong, especially with other men. They had to either win or come off looking good. After all, image is everything! They avoided shame like the plague. These were wounded men who could not tolerate any perceived insult to their fragile esteem.

The new men were out to make an impression, another meager attempt to cover their wounds. They were determined to show the others that being in this group was all a mistake. They were "caught doing what all men do" and were paying the unjust price. They would come to group, pay their fees, and "get through it" like men.

I looked around the room, watching the posturing. I saw the smugness that covered their insecurity. I heard the brash bravado that hid the inner doubts. These were fully grown men, but the little boys inside were not far below the surface. I felt saddened when I thought about the armor each had carried for so long to cover the pain.

Do they really believe all this stuff? I wondered. My job was to engage in discussion with them—honoring them as men, understanding their defense structure, and beginning the slow work of chipping away at their heavy armor.

Defenses to Protect Wounds

As I looked around the room, I was tempted to see only a group of angry men. They were ready to argue with anything I said. Their expressions and postures told me, "You can pretend you are in charge here, but no one tells me what to do or think." The hostility was tangible. My training and experience told me that the room was filled with more than anger. These men were wounded. I have found that people who hurt, hurt people. And so these men had struck out against others in defense of their own vulnerabilities. They had learned how to use power and control tactics. This was what they knew, and it had, at least to some degree, gotten them what they wanted.

I pondered how I would confront them. Experience has taught me that I need to be firm but avoid saying anything to shame them. They had experienced far too much shame already in their lives. How could I gently lift the bandages covering their wounds and apply healing ointment?

"Jim," I said to a husky, balding man in his fifties, "when you talk about using women because they want to be used, do you really believe that's what they want? Or is it possible that other men have used them before, and that's all these women know? I want you to take a moment to consider how the women in your life have responded to your treatment of them. What do you think?"

"I think they get exactly what they ask for. I guess guys have treated them bad before, but they know how to get out of it if they want."

"Do they?" I asked the group. I paused to let them consider the question. "Do women want to be disrespected? What if they just don't know how to change, or are afraid to hope for anything better?"

I looked over at Paul, a short, stout man with a surprisingly strong presence in the group. He had been in the group for nearly a year now and had worked through much of his underlying grief and depression. When the others tossed out their sexist opinions, Paul remained silent. He squirmed in his chair, and I knew he had some opinions about what he was hearing. In previous sessions, he had expressed true regret for his abusive actions with his wife. He had considered his years of partying, abusing his body, and using others for his own satisfaction. Now he spoke into the guarded silence.

"I look back…and I've taken advantage of a lot of women. I did it to make myself feel better. I was depressed and didn't know it. When I think about those women, I realize they were victims even before meeting me. But I didn't help them any, and I sure didn't help myself. Look at my life. I'm on my fourth marriage, and Sheila isn't sure she's going to stay with me. We all need to learn some lessons."

Silence returned as Paul retreated into sadness. I hoped his testimonial would be enough to bring the others around—to help them see that abuse can be subtle or obvious and that no one wins. I wanted them to connect their pain and their violence. That would not be easy, however.

Donald, a recovering alcoholic, didn't accept anything Paul had said. Perhaps it struck too close to home. He wasn't ready to believe that he was abusing anyone or that his life was not working. He was incredibly defensive. Paul's accusation, though indirect, was too much for Donald's rigid ego to incorporate. It was far too threatening. But he knew how to defend himself, and he had used one tactic many times before. He would attack.

Donald pointed his finger at me. "You don't have any idea what it's like out there. You sit up here in your nice office and tell us that we're abusing women. When was the last time you sat on a bar stool at the Sterling Tavern? When was the last time a woman hustled you for a beer? I don't buy that we are the abusers and they are innocent victims. You think men are always the ones in the wrong. You didn't see my wife come at me with closed fists the night I was hauled off to jail."

Donald glared at me. Anger continued to spew from his mouth. He had spent three days in jail and resented it deeply. He could not see how his actions had led to his being incarcerated. He could not see that assault, anytime, with anyone, was wrong and demeaning to himself and others. He could not see how this was partially an expression of underlying pain and sadness. He only knew that he been jailed, and he hated that. He hated being treated like a criminal. He hated being talked to like a criminal by guards who couldn't care less about his story. He hated almost losing the job he had held for 15 years, and he hated the fact that he still could face consequences at work. He hated being strapped for money and having to pay for therapy. He hated.

But Donald did more than hate. He hurt. I could see the tears behind his piercing eyes. He could have cried, but that would have been far too humiliating for him. Others in my group sessions have cried and found acceptance for their loss and grief. But Donald was too new to know how safe this group could be. He would find out in time.

For the next month or two, Donald sparred with me— dodging, weaving, jabbing—using all kinds of maneuvers to avoid having an honest conversation. The tactic is designed to maintain control so no one has to face his issues honestly. It is designed to help men feel powerful. Anytime I got too close to a feeling, Donald avoided the question, attacked my viewpoint, or changed the subject.

Slowly, however, he discovered that these tactics did not work. He found that I would not allow myself to slip into a fight with him. I persisted in bringing him back to a few simple tasks:

- taking responsibility for his part in the patterns of behavior that brought him into the group
- tuning in to his feelings and learning how to label them
- exploring how he might think and behave differently next time
- practicing managing his anger and defensiveness and keeping an open mind whenever possible

As you look at this list, you may be wondering if you can encourage your spouse to practice these strategies. The answer is yes.

A Simple Exercise

One of my goals for the men in my group is for them to learn to identify their feelings and make healthy choices. This is not a simple goal, but it is certainly a worthy one. So many things pertaining to personal and relational growth depend upon the ability to understand feelings. To that end, I start every group with the following exercise: Tell us how you feel, what you think, and what you want.

While this exercise may sound simple, it stumps more than a few men. They desperately want to use one of their vague "feeling" words:

"Fine."

"Okay."

"Good."

"Great."

"Lousy."

"Bad."

Obviously, these monosyllabic responses do not represent refined thinking. They are the stuff that send many women into despair and keep men detached from what is happening inside. As Herb Goldberg says in his book *The Hazards of Being Male,*

> Today, despite often-heard verbalizations to the contrary and an emphasis on feelings which have emerged from the world of encounter and growth groups, there is still a great discomfort and embarrassment when a man overtly and spontaneously expresses his emotions, breaks down in tears, rages in open anger or hate, trembles and shakes in fear, or even laughs too boisterously.[1]

Partners in the Shadows

When I am working with men, I am very aware that their wives and partners are in the shadows. I wonder what life is like for these women. Perhaps you are one of them. Perhaps you live with a man who is filled to the brim with defensiveness. Have you suggested that he attend counseling, only to hear him say, "It not my problem. You go if you need to talk so much"?

Have you confronted him about his irritability, only to have him tell you, "I wouldn't be so uptight if you would just leave me alone. I have a lot on my mind"?

Have you suggested that he consult a doctor for medications, only to hear him say, "I don't need to take any drugs. I need to be clearheaded for my job. Besides, I don't need a crutch to cope"?

Have you prayed for him and asked him to talk with the pastor, only to have him say, "I'm not talking to the pastor, and I don't want you talking to the pastor about our problems. I can handle my own problems. This is between you and me"?

You watch from the shadows. You see the walls he's erected and the moat he's filled to protect himself from you and from any meaningful confrontation with his feelings. As he retreats further into his dark world, you wonder if you can possibly bridge the growing chasm between you.

Unfortunately, as the chasm widens, you feel even more powerless to reach him. Your world becomes smaller and smaller. Like him, you feel angry, misunderstood, hurt, and frustrated. You begin to wonder if he really is the problem or if your own issues may be at the root of things. He is so adept at putting his spin on things that you begin to question yourself.

Let me say this in the most candid terms possible: If you picked up this book out of concern for your spouse, the odds are very high that you accurately perceive a problem. You would not be reading a book like this if the problem didn't exist. Do not allow his defensiveness or his inability to express the softer emotions to deter you from finding the key to the drawbridge that will lead you back to the castle of his heart.

Best Friends?

Denise sat quietly, looking down at the cup of coffee she had brought with her to her counseling appointment. She'd told me that she'd been reluctant to come in because everything felt so discouraging in her marriage. What could a counselor do for her at this late stage?

She was a tidy middle-aged woman. She wore a neatly pressed skirt and blouse. Her nails were painted a soft red, and her gray hair spilled down to her shoulders. She was excessively gentle and spoke haltingly, guarding her words and her feelings.

She felt very guilty for being unsure whether she wanted to work to save the marriage or leave her husband, Greg, for another man. She had met this other man only a few months ago but already felt a stronger emotional connection to him than she did to her husband. She found him to be more open and confident than her husband.

She reflected on her marriage of 30 years—about how it had been so lonely for her and how that loneliness had led to the companionship of another man. I knew she was wondering whether I would judge her for her actions.

"I would never have looked for another man," she said. "I'm not that kind of woman. Married for life. I follow Christian principles. But after all the problems Greg and I have had, I suppose this was inevitable. I used to push so hard for him to talk to me, but he never really did. He just seemed to get quieter and quieter over the years. Nothing I did seemed to help."

Her marriage had not been entirely bad, she said. Initially, it didn't seem bad enough to leave him, let alone seek the company of another man. Adultery was against her moral values, and besides, she had always believed she could get Greg to change. But after so many years, she was just so lonely, she said repeatedly. The early years were painful for her, but she had adjusted to Greg's distance from her. She became somewhat accustomed to the silences in their home by occupying herself with her craft projects and her children's activities. She had joined two study groups, taken craft and sewing classes, and devoted a great deal of time and energy to creating a "project room" in their home. When the children grew up and left home, she went back to college to finish the early education degree she had abandoned years earlier.

Now that the children were grown and living on their own, the distance between Greg and her had begun to wear on her. Even her job as a day-care instructor was not enough to quell the anxieties she felt. And so she came in for counseling.

"Greg is a nice man," Denise shared softly. "He has been a good dad to our three sons. I think I still love him. He has never cheated on me. He has always worked hard. He has been with the same company for 30 years. I'm not sure that I could ask for anything more."

"Except for him to communicate with you?" I said.

"Yes, except that. And to be truly intimate with me."

"What do you mean?"

"Well, the more I think about it, it's not just that he wouldn't talk to me. He's refused to share himself with me in so many ways. He never shared his hurts with me—or his joys. All I ever saw were his moods. The only emotion I ever saw was anger. Never excitement or optimism or playfulness. He's never let himself be vulnerable with me. For goodness' sake, we should be best friends, but we're not."

Denise's irritation began to show. She clenched her fists as she continued to share the emotions she had kept pent up for so long.

"Yes," I said. "Marriage should be a place where you live with your best friend. Men, unfortunately, don't get that. They often won't allow themselves to get close to anyone. Tell me more about how it was with Greg."

"He was always working. He has been a mechanic with the school district for 30 years. He gives everything to that job. If something breaks down, no matter what time of day or even on the weekends, he is there to help. But he won't spend that kind of energy on our marriage. And so I'm left alone even when he is home. He has no friends, and watching television is the only thing he does besides work. Every year he seems a little more sullen and irritable. I think he's depressed, but he will never admit it."

"So, what do you want to do now?" I asked. "You have a husband who has not attended to himself, or you, and another man is showing you attention. You are in a very awkward situation."

"I don't really want to look outside my marriage for the understanding I need. I'm open to suggestions, but I'm also desperate."

An Affair of the Heart

As Greg grew more and more distant from her, Denise began to consider what life might be like with another man. One who was happy, even joyful. What would it be like to be with a person who actually wanted to have a relationship with her? Not surprisingly, when her emptiness met opportunity, a relationship began to blossom.

Denise had given serious consideration to the possibility of leaving Greg. However, she came to see that ending her marriage for another set of problems with another man was not the answer she wanted. She simply wanted to find a way to reach Greg, to develop a fruitful relationship like the one that appeared possible with the other man. We explored how that might be possible.

First, Denise set some firm boundaries on her advancing friendship with the other man. She agreed to quit having lunches and telephone conversations with him. For the time being, she would concentrate her energies on reestablishing a loving relationship with her husband. We agreed that was a great start.

Over the next few months Denise continued in counseling alone. Greg remained steadfast in his belief that he did not need counseling. He became defensive when he perceived her to be challenging him. We clearly had to find a way to deliver a potent message to him in a way that he could hear.

Saying It So He'll Listen

No one likes to be criticized. Because men are reluctant to look into their hearts, when they see an attack coming they run for cover.

You may be able to relate to Denise, who needs some answers about how to reach her husband. Together, Denise and I devised a plan that would give her the best chance of reaching Greg. I call it the Seven Cs Plan. It does not guarantee that a man will lower his defenses, especially if those defenses are ingrained and extremely difficult to penetrate. But this formula stands a good chance of making significant headway.

- *Calm.* Perhaps the most important tactic for getting a man to listen is to go about it calmly. You can give the message emphatically, but it must not include yelling, shaming, or lecturing. This is the surest way to turn a man off and cause him to retreat even further from you.

- *Clarity.* Men need clear information. That means you will need to sit back, collect yourself, and consider carefully what message you want to give to him. Denise rehearsed telling Greg that their marriage was in jeopardy. In fact, she reluctantly decided that she was going to tell Greg about her interest in another man. She knew that this was likely to create turmoil in their relationship, but she hoped that the turmoil would be the catalyst needed to spur both of them to restore their marriage.

- *Conciseness.* Men do not want to be lectured. They want the facts, and they want them concisely. They want to know what is wrong and how to fix the problem. Denise prepared to tell Greg exactly what she needed.

- *Conviction.* Women have a perspective that can be helpful to men and must share it with confidence and conviction. They are committed to relationships, and this can be very helpful to men.

- *Consistency.* Women need to be consistent in their message. You will not help by sharing a problem one day or for one week and then dropping the issue if he resists. He undoubtedly will. Men are not going to change unless they have to. They are not going to give up childish patterns if those patterns are still working for them. So give your message clearly, concisely, and with conviction and consistency.

- *Conciliation.* Your goal is to heal the relationship. Imagine saying to your spouse, "I am telling you this because I love you and want a better relationship. I am not suggesting a divorce—I am committed to you. I am telling you this because I want to be closer and more intimate with you."

- *Consequences.* If your man refuses to listen, even after you have followed constructive guidelines, he needs a consequence. Although this may sound juvenile, consequences have their time and place. They are part of God's order of things. Just as He gave consequences to His promises and commands, we need to attach consequences to our convictions. People will take us far more seriously if we let them know exactly what we need and expect, and what will happen if they ignore our expectations. Those consequences can mean anything from an incisive sharing of emotion to temporary separation.

You are probably reviewing this list and deciding where you are doing well and where you need some improvement. Most people I know, myself included, have not used these communication tools perfectly. We slip and revert to old, destructive methods of communicating. You know what they are. You know that you will do more harm than good if you scold, humiliate, rant and rave, or pout. Withdrawing into silence or getting back at him in passive-aggressive ways will not help. Your best hope of productive communication is to be reasonable and share your expectations in a direct and honest manner.

Grief Is the Healing Feeling

Months later, Denise and Greg came to my office together. The brisk fall afternoon made me wonder if perhaps the seasons were about to change in their marriage as well.

Greg was a tall, slender man with short, gray hair. He wore jeans and a striped work shirt, slightly stained around the cuffs. He walked slowly into the room, pausing to glance around before sitting down. He looked awkward and uncomfortable.

"So, how do you feel about being here?" I asked Greg.

He was silent and sullen. He looked at Denise sternly.

"Well," Denise began. "It's no secret that this was my idea. Greg is not excited about being here."

"Is that right, Greg? You don't want to be here?"

"No. This was Denise's idea. I'm here because she said that if I refused to come she was moving out. What choice did I have?"

"Sounds as if you feel like you were blackmailed into coming."

"What would you call it? She says if I want to save our marriage I have to come to counseling. So, I'm here."

Greg glared at Denise. The tension between them was as thick as the fog rolling over the bay that morning.

Although Greg displayed anger, he also appeared very drawn and sad. He avoided eye contact. Clearly, he was a man in crisis.

"So, you want to save your marriage," I said. "Receiving an ultimatum never feels good. You could have told Denise to forget it. But you didn't. You must care about her and want to save your marriage, or you wouldn't be here. It takes strength to admit that, Greg."

He looked at me for a moment before speaking. His anger had subsided. He settled into the chair and began to relax.

During the next few weeks of counseling, Greg was testy at times, but he gradually lightened up. At first, he said he wanted to solve the problem on his own. I gradually built rapport and helped him see that we had some significant work to do. I found out that he enjoyed reading about World War II, which I also have some interest in, and this forged an initial bond between us, helping us move beyond superficialities and into the deeper areas of the heart.

As the weeks passed, Greg shared more about his upbringing and his current life. Denise watched and offered a few thoughts here and there. She described his symptoms of depression, and after initial resistance, he agreed that he might be depressed. He shared how he had grown up with a distant father and an abusive stepmother. He had learned to guard his emotions, and he was wary of anyone who wanted to get too close. He had learned to live in a sterile world, void of emotions that would make him vulnerable. Slowly, however, he released his pain.

By uncovering his grief, Greg found a release that penetrated his very nature. By honoring his sadness and his wounds, he developed an emotional awareness that helped him connect to Denise in new and exciting ways. She was beginning to sense that Greg really did care about her—enough to work on their marriage and on himself. They still have work to do, but he has found relief from his negative attitude and depression, and he is learning to communicate.

Beneath Greg's tough exterior was a wounded man. The same is true for many men who have buried their wounds beneath years of workaholism, drinking, and distance. They want to avoid pain at all costs. They want to avoid the tears that inevitably come when they venture too close to their wounds. But hope was in the air. Greg was willing to begin facing his wounds, and healing had begun.

Finding Our Heart

Greg began to find his grief and engage in the healing process. As he opened up, he found the path to his sensitive heart as well. Men's specialist Robert Hopcke, author of *Men's Dreams, Men's Healing,* shares many stories about the difficulty of teaching men to become aware of their feelings and trust those feelings as friends, not enemies. He sees men

> treating their difficulties as mechanical problems to be repaired, a process into which the inner life enters not at all. Just as reading books on playing the piano is not quite the same as practicing scales, so, despite all the books on feelings, the vast majority of male clients…have the anesthesia of male socialization.[2]

I recently purchased the book *Wild at Heart* by John Eldrege for my two grown sons. Eldredge contends that men need to find healthy ways to express their manliness. Men have become soft and display their desire for adventure in destructive ways.

My sons and I have spent many hours over the years bonding to each other in "wild" ways. Though they are grown now, they still enjoy a warm hug as much as the touch that comes from wrestling to determine their father's strength. We enjoy a rigorous outing on snowshoes in the Olympic Mountains and the intermittent snowball fight, and we warm up in the hot tub. This is a time to thaw frozen limbs, to be sure, but also a time to thaw frozen emotions. Here we are able to talk man-to-man about things of adult life. I am able to ask them about relationships and emotions, and they ask me some of the same piercing questions. I ask my oldest if he and his girl-friend are considering marriage. I ask my youngest if he is frightened about traveling to Costa Rica alone.

Here, in the waning sunlight, after an exhausting foray into the outdoors, I have my sons' attention, and they have mine. It is a time to laugh but also a time to be vulnerable. I ask them how they are really doing now that they are entering adult life with all its challenges. It is a time to laugh and a time to cry. I so appreciate both.

In a recent discussion with my sons, they commented on how I appeared to need more male companionship. They had known me to be an "adventuresome" guy and noticed that part of my life seemed to be shrinking. They challenged me to develop some friends with whom I could mountain bike, hike, and enjoy other activities.

We had a rousing discussion about the importance of male camaraderie and maintaining the ability to be vulnerable. We are learning now, as men, to admit that we need each other—to share our joys as well as our sorrows. Eldrege warns, "Our sin is that stubbornness part inside that wants, above all else, to be independent. There's a part of us fiercely committed to living in a way where we do not have to depend on anyone—especially God."[3]

Lazarus

Jesus is a wonderful example of a man's man. As we follow His life, we see His character unfold through His many relationships. He treated women with dignity and respect. In John 4:7 we read of a Samaritan woman (whom the Jews would have despised) coming to a well and Jesus asking her to get Him a drink. The woman was surprised that a Jew would ask her for a drink. Jesus proceeded to have a discussion with her, asking about her life. He knew she had been married five times and was not married to the man with whom she was living. He did not shame her but used the opportunity to tell her about "living water."

As a psychologist, I am impressed to see how wholeheartedly Jesus experienced and expressed a wide range of emotions. His life was anything but mundane.

Think of the camaraderie Jesus must have felt with the 12 men who lived and traveled with Him for three years, and especially with His inner circle—Peter, James, and John ("the disciple whom Jesus loved"). When He was tired, He wanted to be alone with them (Mark 6:31). Was it because He felt alone that He wanted to reveal His true nature to them (Matthew 17:1-9)? He was "full of joy through the Holy Spirit" when 72 of His disciples returned from a preaching tour (Luke 10:21), and He was openly disappointed when the 12 were slow to believe (Matthew 17:17; Mark 16:14).

Jesus was thrilled with the faith of a centurion and of a Gentile woman (Luke 7:9; Matthew 15:28), and He wept over the city that would not respond to His love (Luke 13:34). He burned with anger at religious hypocrisy and oppression (John 2:14-16), and He welcomed little children into His arms (Mark 10:13-16). He approached His passion with apprehension (Luke 12:50), and He needed the support of His friends as He searched His soul for the strength to accomplish His mission (Mark 14:33-34).

One story especially shows Jesus' sorrow. The story of Lazarus in John 11:1-45 shows a vulnerable side to Jesus. We know little about Lazarus, but we know that he and his sisters, Mary and Martha, were Jesus' friends. The sisters sent word to Jesus one day and said, "Lord, the one you love is sick." The story goes on to say that Lazarus died, and his sisters were very distressed. Jesus joins them in their time of grief, "groaning in his spirit." We read, in the shortest verse in the Bible, a poignant and powerful statement: *Jesus wept.* He had the courage to cry even though He knew that He would soon raise Lazarus from the dead. He was caught up in the community of the grief-stricken and allowed Himself to be fully present to His friends and their pain.

This story is remarkable because it allows us to see Jesus' full humanity. Even though He had an eternal perspective and could easily have defended Himself against the more painful elements of life, He chose to live fully in the moment.

Courage

Being a real man takes courage. On the other hand, nothing is particularly courageous about being shallow and unwilling to share your vulnerabilities. I do not find anything virtuous about drinking away pain, working oneself to death, or acting as if things are fine when we are crying inside. Courage comes from being able to admit, against the grain of masculine culture, that all is not well and that we do not have all the answers. It means being able to talk straight to the women in our lives about our sadness and our losses, and to allow them to share in our victories and failures.

As you continue to read about men and their blues, I hope that you will maintain the fortitude to lovingly demand that the men in your life deal with their struggles head-on. You can insist that they strive toward true masculinity, which means courageously facing grief and sadness directly. You will have to avoid picking up the pieces for them or turning away as they shirk their God-given responsibilities.

I hope and trust that you are willing to do that.

chapter
4

When Did It Start?
Childhood Influences

If you lose hope, you lose the vitality that keeps life moving.
You lose that courage to be, that quality that helps you go on in
spite of it all. And so today I still have a dream.

—MARTIN LUTHER KING, JR.

SETH SMELTZ WAS A QUIET, GANGLY BOY who was painfully aware
that he came from the poorer side of town. He grew up like
most of the other kids in the Fairway District. Their fathers
worked at the mills and scraped out a living from hard, physical labor. They attended the neighborhood church and knew
the minister as Pastor Bill.

The rich kids went to school across town, and their families lived up on the hill overlooking the city. Their fathers were
managers at the mills or worked at the hospital as doctors,
nurses, or technicians. They were members of the large community church that all the important people in town attended.

Seth envied these families and loathed them. He had it
rougher than they did. But he also had a toughness that came
from knowing the rules of the street and was able to make his
own decisions and defend himself when necessary. Although

he wasn't afraid to fight, he preferred the safer sanctuary of books and video games.

The Fairway District was known for breeding tough, difficult kids. Family income was low to moderate, houses were simple, fathers were generally absent, and drugs were readily available. Still, Seth was able to keep his nose clean. Other kids his age were spending time in juvenile detention, but Seth knew how to avoid getting "sucked into the system," as they called it. Once in the "system," many never got out. He would rather read about the challenges of life and had acquired a taste for Steinbeck, Verne, and Hemingway. That was unusual, he told me, for someone who came from "the District."

Not only were financial times challenging, but Seth's social development also had its ups and downs. During his early childhood, the other kids teased Seth and called him Seth Smelly instead of Seth Smeltz. He winced inwardly, but he kept his pain to himself. He didn't even tell his parents what was happening on the school grounds. Inside he vowed to overcome it—if not with brawn, then with brains. His skin grew a little thicker with each year, his emotions buried somewhere beneath the growing layers.

Seth also had to contend with skin problems as a child. He had eczema and often broke out in rashes. The other children taunted him even more during these times, suggesting sarcastically that he needed to take a bath. Doctors offered little assistance. They said that he simply needed to take care of his skin and that he would eventually outgrow the problems he was having. In the meantime, their medical counsel did little to soothe his emotional pain or heal his skin. He tried nearly every salve and quick-fix remedy, without notable results.

Seth spent more time alone when life became difficult. He sometimes coped with the teasing by standing up for himself, but usually he just isolated himself in his room. His mother tried to coax him out to be with the family, but he always had a book to finish or a video game to play. All the while, he struggled with self-esteem.

I learned about his childhood problems, and those that followed him into adulthood, as he sat in my office years later.

He sat quietly, looking out the window. He was an unusual man in that he had come in with his wife for marriage counseling and then asked to come in and talk alone about his past. His decision wasn't exactly spontaneous—his wife had told him repeatedly that he needed to come to terms with his past for both of their sakes. She had separated from him weeks earlier and told him he had to change to save their four-year marriage. She had told him what many women are saying to their husbands—"You need to work on your life. You are difficult to live with!" He knew she was right and made several appointments.

Seth was a rangy man of about 30. He had a day's worth of stubble on his face as well as a neatly groomed goatee. He was already balding and shaved his head. He wore brown Carhartt overalls with a hooded sweatshirt fraying around the sleeves. He politely took off his cap with the logo from Cummins, where he worked as a diesel mechanic.

"So, where do we start, Doc?" he finally said, with a boyish grin. He had a "let's get to it" attitude that was not unusual for a man. "Can't say I've ever done anything like this before. Do you want to hear some things about my childhood that might be worth talking about?"

"Sure, Seth. Your wife said she thinks that's where some things went wrong for you. Maybe that's where we can begin, and then we can go from there."

Seth began to tell me about his childhood, about the teasing, the fights, the struggle to find acceptance, his love of books, and how he thought life had been all right—until he reached adolescence. He felt good about his family life and his three younger siblings—until his parents suddenly divorced when he was 12.

"One night my dad came into my room and told me he had something to talk to me about. I had no idea what was coming. He looked at me, big tears in his eyes, and said that he would be moving out that night. He and Mom were getting a divorce. I couldn't believe it. I didn't know what that meant. I didn't know what to ask him, and he didn't know what to tell me. Two hours later he was gone."

"You remember that night like it was yesterday, don't you?"

"Yup. I can still picture my dad crying and see him leaving the driveway. I don't know what happened to me, but I haven't really been happy since that time. It's like any air that was in my balloon just left."

"That was a huge loss to you. Who wouldn't be upset if their parents divorced, ruining the life you had going?"

"My mom and dad never talked to us kids. I still don't know why it happened. All I know is that I've been irritated with them and—although I can't explain why—even with myself ever since. I don't trust anyone, and I can see that I'm not easy to live with. I sit alone and read more than ever before. I don't really talk to my wife, and I make excuses not to be with the few friends I have. And I'm afraid my wife is going to divorce me. She doesn't seem to love me anymore. I wonder if she's right about me being depressed. Is it possible that I have been depressed ever since I was a kid?"

Seth appeared tired and hopeless. Dark circles rimmed his eyes. When I commented on his apparent sadness, he quickly shifted the topic to his job, stating that he had been working a lot lately. I let the obvious avoidance go, as if unnoticed.

"All I know how to do is work. I put in my 40 hours and another 20 sometimes. That's what my dad taught us kids—to work. I don't like to work this hard, but it's an easy way to make some extra money," he said, glancing out the window. Then he looked up at me with a half-smile. "I'm proud that I can work so hard and earn so much. I want to give my kids things I didn't get. I want them to have nice clothes, like I never had. And birthdays are important to me, since I got next to nothing after my parents divorced. My kids aren't going to go through what I went through, that's for sure."

"How does Becky feel about your working so much?"

"She doesn't like it. She thinks it makes me irritable and harder on the kids. I think she has a point. I'm listening more these days."

This is Seth's second marriage, and he wants to save it if possible. He knows that he has to understand some of his destructive character traits and his depression in order to save the marriage. Becky gave him an ultimatum that he must change. If he does, she has suggested, she may be motivated to keep working on their marriage.

"I don't like her threats," he said to me during a subsequent session. "But I think she's right. I can be a jerk and I know it. I know that I have a bad temper and can be impatient with the kids. When she asked me to leave, I wanted to tell her that I was finished with the marriage. That's what I would have done ten years ago, but not now. It's time for me to look at myself closely. So that's your job, Doc."

Seth was courageous to be sitting here, willing to look into the experiences of the past that had given way to the irritable, angry, and depressed man in my office.

Seven years ago, after the breakup of his first marriage, Seth's solution had been to run. But, he said jokingly, "You can run, but you can't hide." Now it was time to take a look at how he came to be depressed and make some changes so that he and his marriage stood a chance of survival.

In addition to his willingness to attend counseling, Seth displays other hints of hopefulness. Though he feels deflated and frightened, he believes that God can open his heart and release the years of accumulated pain. He is not sure how that will happen, but he has used this crisis to get in touch with his former pastor and has started attending church again. He wants God to lift away the anger and resentment he feels in his heart. It is a wonderful beginning.

Sad and Angry Boys

Kids are not supposed to have serious problems. Their lives are supposed to be carefree. As parents, we want to protect them and create magical worlds for them to play in and explore. That is, after all, their "job"—to learn about their world. We certainly don't want them to start life carrying a bag of troubles that can grow and become overwhelming. Unfortunately, their world, like yours, is not perfect. Adult problems find their way down to children, and too often, kids start life with troubles too big for them to handle.

As Seth and I talked about his childhood, I saw some predisposing factors that led to his adult depression. Many causes of depression in men started when they were boys. Let's look more closely at Seth's life and some experiences that set him up for depression, noting the patterns that may fit your husband as well.

Significant Loss

Seth had experienced significant losses during his childhood, culminating in the loss of a stable family life. Even prior to the end of his parents' marriage, Seth lived in a home with limited finances. We do not know the full extent of the financial problems, but Seth said that his father had to work long hours to make ends meet. His father was absent from many of Seth's activities and did not play a large role in family life.

Seth also struggled with medical problems that affected him socially. He lived with his eczema in silence. He retreated into classic books to help him cope with his social problems. His stories provided a safe world when things got bad.

Finally, we get a glimpse into Seth's parents' divorce and the pain it caused. They not only ended their marriage but also did it in a terribly destructive way. They didn't talk about the process with the children. The children did not know what was happening or what to expect in the future. They did not have anyone with whom to share their grief.

William Pollack, in *Real Boys Workbook,* discusses the issues involved for boys whose parents divorce. He notes that many boys face grief with a stiff upper lip, a behavior that our society reinforces. He offers examples:

> The stoic face of Prince Harry after his mother, Princess Diana, died, and three-year-old John F. Kennedy, Jr.'s poignant salute before his father's coffin, were applauded by the press and public as signs of these young boys' strength, and even heroism. But the traditional "stiff upper lip" of manhood keeps boys from dealing with their grief in the natural ways that will eventually heal their pain.[1]

Many boys shoulder additional burdens when a loss in the family occurs, and this was the case for Seth. Because he was the oldest, he felt responsible to be "the man of the house." His mother asked him to help care for his younger siblings, to shield them from the loss of their father. This burden, however, only added to his own pain. He now had even more reason to hide his vulnerable feelings of grief, fear, and loss.

Internalized Anger

Women sense, and rightly so, that many men are essentially angry, hotheaded, and ready to fight at a moment's notice. As you ride in your husband's car, how often does he treat the road as if it were the Indianapolis 500, a race that he must win at all costs? How often do you find yourself wondering, *Do you have to drive this way?* This is more than male competitiveness. Men constantly seem to be on the verge of anger. The actions of other drivers, crazy as they may be, cannot account for the fire in men's bellies.

Seth told me that he was angry with his parents, not only for divorcing, but also for the way that they did it. He spent years struggling to make sense out of that event. Why did his parents divorce? Why didn't they warn the children or talk to them about it after the divorce?

Seth has been justifiably angry about this situation for a long time. His mother and father are still alive, but Seth says that he has little to do with them. He cannot forgive them for what they did to him and his siblings. One minute they seemed to be a fairly happy family—attending church and going on family vacations—and the next he was living with his mother as she struggled to meet their financial responsibilities. Church participation vanished.

Seth is particularly angry at his father. He has heard, in bits and pieces, that his father may have been unfaithful to his mother and that this may have precipitated the divorce. He has never had the courage to ask either parent if this is true, but he believes it is possible. He sees his parents occasionally, but Seth has never repaired the emotional breach that occurred when they divorced.

Seth tells me that he often feels consumed by anger. It rarely leaves him, and he wonders why he feels this way. His anger is a constant weight on his shoulders. He has no effective release, which is true for many men.

Anger, undirected or expressed, can lead to depression. A vicious circle develops—anger leads to feelings of guilt, feelings of inadequacy, conflict with spouses, and more feelings of anger. In the end, all that is left is anger and discouragement.

Distrust

Let's think about the effects of trust and distrust. How do you feel when you have a group of friends with whom you feel free to share your thoughts and emotions? Envision a community of kindred spirits who encircle you, think about you, care about you and what you are feeling, and will not betray your confidence.

Now picture it all evaporating. Imagine the friends are gone, the confidence they gave you is gone, the caring community they provided is gone, and the trust and confidentiality are gone.

Seth does not truly trust anyone. Sure, he had a wife who cared about him. But Becky also said that she will leave him if he does not change. She will leave him just as his last wife left him. This threat is very real to Seth. He thinks about it and feels its weight every day. He knows that he must change, but changing is not that easy. He understands his wife's position but resents her for it at the same time.

Distrust is a precursor to depression because it creates loneliness. When Seth feels that he cannot share his feelings with anyone, when he thinks no one really cares, he locks himself up in a world that is akin to self-imposed solitary confinement. This world becomes the breeding ground for depression.

Rejection

As much as Seth tried to not take his parents' divorce personally, it felt intensely personal to him. When Seth's father left, Seth was crushed. Even though his relationship with his father was less than perfect, Seth still adored him. When his father left his mother, he left Seth too.

Seth has carried his father's rejection for many years. He did not see his father very often after the divorce and has resented his father for that. Because he was a youngster, he did not understand why his father didn't make more of an effort to be involved in his life. His father has offered vague explanations for being absent—such as not wanting to talk to his mother—but they never made much sense to Seth. It was all very confusing, and the rejection has weighed heavily on his self-esteem.

Prior to the divorce, Seth held onto a bit of hope that his father would eventually make himself available emotionally and physically. After the divorce his hopes faded.

Richard Rohr and Joseph Martos, in their marvelous book *The Wild Man's Journey: Reflections on Male Spirituality,* talk about the wounds that boys suffer from their fathers. A primary wound comes from rejection. "A son needs to believe that his father respects and even admires him. As a boy he wants his daddy to be proud of him, but as he grows toward manhood a father's pride can seem very patronizing to him. What he needs all along is not only parental approval but adult respect and honest admiration."[2]

Counseling has helped Seth understand what happened in his parents' marriage—as best as we could sort things out. We have not been able to put all of the pieces together, but at least we are talking about them. That is something you can do to help your man as well. Keep giving him opportunities to talk about the losses and rejection, and help him understand what happened.

Critical Parenting

Many children grow up with critical fathers. Young boys who experience this criticism become equally critical with themselves and others. As men, they are not fun to be with because they are so negative.

Seth remembers his father being a demanding man. Although he was gone much of the time, he expected a lot of Seth when he was around. He expected Seth to watch over his siblings when his parents were gone, an assignment Seth hated. He also expected Seth to get good grades and do myriad chores around the house. Seth wanted to please his father and felt bad when he disappointed his parents.

Like Seth, I was raised by a critical father. I love him very much and am thankful he is alive to play an active role in my life. But I won't deny that he was critical. He was critical because his father was critical. His father was critical because his father was critical—and so it goes. Men learn to be critical by example, and the cycle continues until it is broken.

Critical parents beget inner criticism, feelings that one will never measure up. I must struggle to silence the lies of my inner critic:

- You are not working hard enough.
- You are not giving enough to others.
- You do not compare favorably to other men.
- You are not achieving enough.

The problem with the inner critic is not only that it is not rational but also that it never shuts up. The inner critic has a voracious appetite and always seems to want more and more of my soul. Like most men, I must learn to silence the inner critic and love myself unconditionally. I must remember that being enough has nothing to do with outer accomplishments but is rather a state of being. This is hard work and requires loving attention. I am always on the lookout for the inner critic's irrational expectations. This is also a spiritual matter. I am enough because I am God's creation. I am a human being, not a human doing.

I have heard people say that seeing our heavenly Father as a loving God is difficult if we have not had a loving father of our own. Picturing God as a critical father is certainly easy, and it creates all kinds of problems. If we project rigid criticism onto our heavenly Father, we are likely to lead a life filled with shoulds and oughts and fears of punishment. Healing comes when we are able to see Father God as a loving parental figure, one who cares deeply about us and wants the best for us.

I am thankful that my father has softened incredibly over the years. He has mellowed as he has aged and truly regrets being as harsh as he was for many years. With a great deal of reparenting, I have learned to accept his love and incorporate that as a model for "parenting" myself. I have also learned to be a softer father to my own two sons.

Feeling Misunderstood

After the divorce, Seth proceeded to detach himself from everyone. He was already somewhat distant from others, and the divorce rocked his boat. He felt that he could no longer trust his mother or his father. It is no surprise, given this distance and detachment, that Seth did not feel understood. We feel very alone when "no one understands."

Seth's wife, Becky, once shared her confusion with me. "If he wants to be understood, why does he keep pushing me away? If he wants to be accepted, why is he so critical of me?" These, of course, are very good questions.

Dr. Herb Goldberg, author of *The Hazards of Being Male,* acknowledges that men are frightened of their dependency on women. He says that the shallowness we often see in men is really a natural self-protection against excessive dependency. "The male resists closeness and dependency on the female because once the unconscious defense is penetrated by a woman he becomes profoundly attached to the point of deep and almost total dependency."[3]

Goldberg would say, as would many others, that Seth is on a self-destructive path, setting himself up to be misunderstood. He pushes Becky away because he fears becoming too dependent on her. When he entered into marriage, he, like many men, surrendered his other friendships, which also set him up to feel alienated and misunderstood.

Lack of Awareness

The epidemic of boys and men who are strangers to their emotions is remarkable. Because they learn to keep a stiff upper lip, to grin and bear it and "never let them see you hurt," boys and men are often strangers to friends and family. But they cannot help it.

Seth could not do anything about his father working long hours, the financial struggles, the social discomfort. He had no way of fending off the pain that came as a tsunami without warning. His only coping tool was to retreat into a world of books and imagination. There he found a bit of respite from the pain. But in this lonely world, he failed to learn lessons about feelings.

No one was there for Seth to help him learn these things. In fact, no one helps most boys or men learn about feelings, so they are often incapable of sharing thoughts and emotions with their spouse.

Isolation and Loneliness

As the years went by, Seth became more absorbed in his books and more secure in the comfort of his room. During his adolescent years, his mother admonished him to come out of his "dungeon" to be with the family. When he was a young man, his wife essentially did the same thing. She tried to get him to come out of his world of books and work to really be with her and their children.

Unfortunately, Seth established patterns as a youth that he must overcome as an adult. He still tends to retreat in the face of adversity, much to the consternation of his wife. He will now need to practice coming out of his den and socializing with his family.

Social Discomfort

One of the many barriers for men attempting to overcome their blues is their social discomfort, which leaves them isolated and alone. This can be hard for many women to understand, given their propensity for communication and relationships. Women are relationally oriented, but this is often not the case with men. Men are more comfortable in the world of machines and ideas than the world of relationships.

Most men need to venture out and find ways to overcome their discomfort. Seth had to overcome his discomfort with his skin problems. He had to find ways to rise above this external issue and build his confidence. Each person has his or her area of oversensitivity that he or she can and must overcome.

The task is not to join a particular social club but to find places to be utterly transparent. This can be excruciating for some men, but they must discover those places and relationships where they can talk candidly about what is not working in their lives. They must be able to say, "My life is a mess" and not feel ashamed. They must be able to ask for help and not lose face.

This is a major issue for most men, and they often need the help of women to accomplish it. A spouse's support in reestablishing a social life can be a tremendous help.

Restoring Broken Dreams

Watching your spouse struggle under the burden of discouragement he has carried for much of his life can be incredibly frustrating. You see the armor—the terrible losses, the lack of support, the lack of friendship, the excessive work, the broken dreams—yet much of the time, nothing you say makes a difference.

Though you cannot alter your husband's childhood, you can help him gain a new perspective on that experience. Someone has said, "It's never too late to have a happy childhood." Let's discuss how that can happen and how helpful that can be to him.

In previous chapters, you have learned how to talk to him more effectively. Now let's talk about creating a climate of understanding and support in the home that will help him heal. What are some ways that you can help him bounce back from the early problems that led to his adult depression?

Understanding the Loss of the Dream

All children have dreams. If you ask them what they want, they will reveal dreams filled with possibilities. Most of us refuse to dash their hopes. We want them to reach for the sky—to dream of being a famous scientist, a respected author, a star athlete who lands a million-dollar contract. Who are we to tell them that the odds are stacked against them?

Those who have had the misfortune of being raised in an impoverished home know the pain of having their dreams crushed. They know the sinking feeling of their parents' divorce, of moving to a cramped apartment with no yard, of wearing hand-me-down clothes. To recover from these losses, one must understand them, grieve about them, and learn to move on. This was the task for Seth.

As the partner of a man who has a history of losses and has probably begun to personalize them—"bad things always happen to me"—you are in a position to help him separate dysfunctional thinking from clear, biblical thinking. You are able to help him see that the things that happened to him as a child were...

- beyond his control
- not meant for him personally
- unfortunate, but not devastating
- sad, but not overwhelming
- helpful in making him a stronger man
- allowed into our lives for our good

Men who have troubled histories as children need help in gaining a new perspective. You have the power to help your husband gain that fresh viewpoint.

Don't be surprised if your comments initially meet with something less than enthusiasm. He may be defensive at first, but you will be able to use the communication skills we have talked about to reach him. He still may resist your efforts and may have reasons for hanging onto old, destructive beliefs. This may be the time when the two of you need to seek professional help.

Grieving the Loss of the Dream

Grief may be the central ingredient in the healing feeling. Why? Because men have buried their feelings of loss and grief beneath layers of experiences, defense mechanisms, and avoidance tactics. Men will do just about anything to avoid the vulnerability associated with sadness and grief. However, these things hold the key to unlocking a man's inner self. When he is able to loosen the chains around his grief-stricken heart, he is often able to move forward.

Sam Keen, noted author of *Inward Bound,* tells us that the road to recovery lies in learning to suffer with dignity. "Loneliness, loss, disappointment, failure, dis-ease are inevitable. The price of trying to avoid the unavoidable is illusion, or neurosis."[4] All of us experience losses, but healthy people learn to face these losses. That is the royal road to unthawing emotions, both positive and negative—by facing the losses head-on.

How can you help your man face his losses and grieve them in an honest way?

First, you must be comfortable with loss yourself. You must cultivate the ability to sit with sadness. You may be tempted to intellectualize the losses, as he has done for years, but that is not really dealing with them. That is like wearing an antiseptic gown when entering the room of a sick person. Start by daring to come into the room, even if you do not touch. Then learn to touch your man where he hurts.

Second, you can help him find the words to describe his pain and loss. As you might with one of your children, you can use feeling language to talk about the loss. "I know that it had to hurt when your dad walked in suddenly and said that he was leaving. Without any warning or ability to prepare, you suddenly had to make a huge adjustment. And then you had to learn to live with your mom on far less income. That must have been rough."

Third, you can watch for "echoes" of the loss. Watch for other opportunities to talk to him about his pain. Watch for other experiences that might be similar to those in his present or past. Watch for the windows of opportunity where he might be more available to talk about disturbing emotions. Be prepared to talk to him about his feelings. Use feeling language.

These are powerful steps and can be extremely helpful. You are in an influential role with him and can be very helpful if you will be patient. You cannot force this language on him, but you can create a climate where he can naturally share his feelings.

Visualize the New Dream

Thankfully, every lost dream brings the possibility of a new dream. Every act of creation, as Picasso said, is preceded by an act of destruction.

Depression is a deceiver of possibilities. It is like a wet blanket on the dreams of life. When we have the blues, nothing looks possible. If anything can go wrong, we imagine that it will. Hopeless, helpless, hapless. If you have been around a depressed man for very long, you are acquainted with these thoughts and feelings. If you are not careful, some of these discouraging beliefs and emotions can rub off onto you.

Fortunately, the story does not end there. As his helpmate, you are in a position to help him see new possibilities. Becky was able to confront Seth and insist that he get professional help if he wanted to save their marriage, which he did. Most men do. Women will sometimes need to be very matter-of-fact with their spouses—"You must let the doctor check you for depression. This is not optional if you want me to stay here and be supportive of you."

Having begun the process of professional counseling, you can also, when appropriate, help him visualize the new dream. You can help him see that he actually can accomplish the things he wants to. You can encourage him to take classes to advance his career, to join the gym to work on his physical fitness, to create new friendships, to become active in church and flex his spiritual muscles.

Men who are deflated and discouraged need cheerleaders. Spouses are in a good position to offer tempered support and encouragement. This will go a long way toward lifting him out of the blues and on to brighter days. He needs you more than he may let you know.

Getting the emotions jump-started is a very effective way to escape the blues. Emotion, or energy in motion, can help you get the blood flowing again and regain control of your life. God created us as emotional creatures, and that emotion will often lead us where we want and need to go. Iyanla Vanzant, author of *Up from Here,* says, "Emotion is the energy that moves us. In fact, the very word emotion has motion in it. The investment that you put into your emotional being determines if you move, when you move, and why you move."[5]

A Man of Many Dreams

Staying the course in spite of setbacks is one sign of resilience and mental health. However, most of us are a bit more fragile than that. When something or someone waylays us, we can fall into moodiness and even depression. Who of us has not been deflated when life throws us a wicked curveball? Who has not become disconsolate when our dreams have been thwarted?

You may remember the story of Joseph, the youngest son of Jacob. As the story goes (Genesis 37–45), Joseph was born into a privileged position: Jacob loved Joseph more than he loved his other sons. To make matters worse, Joseph reported back to his father about some bad things his brothers were doing. Talk about setting the stage for some rivalry.

The story continues with Joseph having a dream about his privileged position and then indiscriminately flaunting it before his brothers. As you can imagine, this did not set well with them. Their father's partiality and Joseph's cockiness so rankled the brothers that they decided to kill him. But for one brother's intervention and God's protection, he might have died.

Imagine Joseph's thoughts. His dreams suggested to him that he would rise to a favored position in the family. How would he communicate that to his family? Was he comfortable assuming the role of leader? My suspicion is that Joseph was uncomfortable in that position. It certainly set him at odds with his brothers.

Imagine the feelings of the brothers. They watched as their kid brother took a favored role. The sibling rivalry must have been intense. They proceeded to throw him into a pit and left him to die.

Imagine Jacob's feelings as well. His favored son is presumed dead. We read that Jacob ripped his clothes in anguish and frustration. He sobbed and grieved over his lost son. Talk about a series of dreams being destroyed!

Although Joseph did not die, he was sold into slavery—hardly the position that he had dreamt about, hardly the position of royalty he had envisioned for his future. Joseph must have doubted the validity of his dreams. He was destined to be in a position of leadership, and now he found himself sold as a slave. I'm sure Joseph hoped that his father would come looking for him, and when no one came, he must have felt deflated and depressed.

We can imagine that Joseph, after years of separation from his family, must have experienced all the feelings of depression. He was rejected, abandoned, separated from his family, and living in a foreign land. However, Joseph does not let circumstances completely dictate his mood or his destiny. He certainly must have felt discouraged for a time, but he did not let these events spoil his dream. He had a date with destiny, and through God's help, he kept his eye on his goal.

After interpreting Pharaoh's dreams, Joseph becomes a powerful ruler over all of Egypt. He helps to heal the land from a horrible famine. Through circumstances associated with the famine, he is reunited with his father and reconciled with his brothers. Joseph's dreams are restored to a level beyond his imagination.

Reclaiming Your Man's Dreams

You have watched as your man slipped into depression. Perhaps you can see the circumstances that have set him up to become so discouraged. You can see how one block, placed upon another, has created a wall between him and his dreams. He may be dispirited, but he can still have hope. Breaking through that wall may be hard, but you can reach him.

Your husband needs your help. You can play an important role in his healing by being a helpmate to him. Although he may have given in to the circumstances around him, he, like Joseph, can rise above them and reclaim the joy he deserves. You are in a position to help your man reclaim his lost dreams. In fact, you may have to reclaim them for him until he is able to do so for himself. You can believe in him, offering hope when he feels dejected.

In the remaining chapters, we will discuss more tools that you can use to help him recover his lost dreams and the joy that is missing from his life.

chapter
5

Working Man's Blues

I don't like work—no man does—but I like what is in work:
the chance to find yourself.

—Joseph Conrad

Terry CAME TO SEE ME AFTER HIS DOCTOR referred him because of high blood pressure. The problem had been building for the past year, and the doctor decided Terry needed to consider how stress might be impacting the problem. Terry was a modest, slender man who was neatly dressed in khakis and a polo shirt.

Right out of college, Terry had jumped at the chance to work as a software engineer for a new start-up company. He had high expectations after hearing about the company from its recruiters at the university. They were aggressively pursuing the best and brightest engineers, and he felt proud to have landed a job with them. He had been with them now for a few years.

His youthful enthusiasm left him unprepared for some of the company's unspoken expectations. He was joining a cadre of talented, energetic workers who were competing ferociously with giants in the industry. In order to gain a foothold in the marketplace, they would need to work hard—very hard. The company expected Terry to give whatever was needed to ensure success. Terry thought he was up to the task. The work would be hard but the payoffs enormous. The company promised bonuses when workers met or exceeded goals, and profit-sharing options held even more possibilities. His adrenaline was pumping.

Terry's wife, Rene, was not quite as eager to leave college and immerse herself in a high-pressure job. Like Terry, Rene had gone to school and studied computer engineering. After graduation, a company with a reputation similar to the one that had recruited Terry had hired her. Rene was not naive about software start-ups or the demands they made of their employees. She understood the high cost up-front and wonderful possibilities for financial growth along the way. However, she made up her mind that she would not cross certain limits. She would not allow the demands of the company to leave her without a personal life. She had made a conscious effort to continue her book study group as well as her aerobics classes with friends.

Terry and Rene were young—in their mid twenties. They had dated for two years and then married one year ago, not long after landing their new jobs. They had gone from living modestly on school loans and part-time jobs to enjoying a comfortable lifestyle financed by two healthy incomes.

During their college years, when they were dating, they had a wonderful social life. They both enjoyed outdoor activities with friends that included downhill skiing in the winter and water-skiing in the summer. A group of friends often gathered at a friend's cabin on the lake for a weekend of fun. Those days seemed a distant past now.

For a few years, things went very well. They bought new cars, rented a nice apartment with a view of the bay, and spared little expense in refurbishing their wardrobes. Suddenly, their combined earnings neared six figures. Not bad for a couple of twenty-somethings. Their income was more than their parents had made at any time in their careers. They were understandably proud of their accomplishments.

While Rene maintained a fairly traditional work schedule with occasional overtime, Terry was expected to work ten to twelve hours, six days a week. Whenever the company was working on a new version of a software program, the schedule was even more rigorous. All hands were expected to be on deck until they worked out the bugs and the program was ready to ship.

Quite suddenly, Terry and Rene's afternoon meetings at the coffee shop were gone. Gone too were relaxed matinee viewings of the latest movie. Gone were the activities and adventures that had created an electric connection between the two of them.

Terry was tense when he walked into my office. He fidgeted with a cell phone, which he juggled in his right hand. Not surprisingly, it was a combination cell phone and data organizer. He looked like a guy who needed every organizational advantage. He excused himself for a moment as he punched buttons and checked something before returning his attention to me.

"So, Terry. Tell me what brought you here."

"My doctor says I have high blood pressure, which is apparently pretty unusual for someone my age. He wanted me to see someone, though I'm not sure this is necessary. He tried to control the problem with diet, but that doesn't seem to be working. I really don't want to have to be on medication."

"Yes, I can understand that. There are sometimes complications with that kind of medication."

He again looked down at his gadget, then looked up, waiting for my response. "I'm curious about your toy," I said. "It looks like it slices, dices, and answers calls too."

He proudly held it out for my inspection.

"It's a Treo. It organizes data, accepts and sends e-mails, and functions as a cell phone. Wouldn't know what to do without it. It's my brains."

"That's some tool," I said. "Just what every man needs. Now, let's talk a bit about what your doctor found. High blood pressure in a physically fit person of your age really is unusual. I'm guessing he thinks it might be related to something happening in your personal life. Am I close?"

"Yeah. He thinks I might be burning the candle at both ends. He's worried about my marriage, too, though I think he's overreacting."

"Can we talk about it?" I asked.

"Sure, but I don't know that there's a lot to talk about."

Terry and I spent the next two sessions discussing his life. Not surprisingly, it was packed with stress. While his brain was translating it as excitement and action, his body was saying to slow down. His brain was telling him to keep the jets firing at all times, but his body was saying, "Too much."

Terry was not especially motivated to change his life, but in spite of his initial denials, his doctor's concerns had clearly frightened him. Terry was open to the possibility of learning to reduce his stress level. Although he wanted to maintain his current pace at work, he could see that he might have to alter some things if he was to stay healthy for the long run. He was truly torn. He wanted to earn the big bucks, pull down the bonuses for work above and beyond the call of duty, and climb the ladder in pay and responsibility. But he also wanted to stay healthy. He had taken good care of his body prior to going to work, and he wanted to find some kind of balance again.

We had a good conversation about his free time and his relationship with his wife. He admitted that he had little free time anymore for fishing or mountain biking. He conceded that he and his wife had not been on a date in months, and in fact, they had been fighting more than usual recently.

Terry also admitted, rather reluctantly, that work had become less exciting for him. It had become just a job—a place to put in time and get a paycheck. The more hours he worked, the less enthusiasm he had. Much of his initial passion for the job had evaporated.

Near the end of the first visit, I did a brief mental health screening of Terry, with the following results:

- He had been sleeping poorly.

- He worried excessively about work and unfinished projects.

- He had lost ten pounds in the past three months.

- He had abandoned many of his hobbies.

- He no longer associated with friends.

- He often felt irritable, especially with his wife.

After a few sessions, I asked if we might invite Rene to join us. Terry agreed, though he seemed surprised by the request. As it turned out, Rene called and asked to meet alone with me one time before meeting jointly with Terry. Rene was a petite woman, confident and energetic, but far more composed than Terry. She entered my office and went right for the antique rocker. "Just like my grandma's," she said smiling. Without skipping a beat she began.

"I want to talk about Terry, if that's okay. That's why I wanted to see you first before the three of us got together. Terry probably hasn't told you a lot of things you need to know if you're going to help him. I'm willing to be here and talk in front of him, but I would be a little more comfortable sharing them with you alone first."

"That's fine. Why don't you go ahead? I'll ask questions if I'm not clear about something."

Rene explained her concerns about her husband. She was afraid that Terry would not be candid with me. Telling the truth would make him look weak. Also, she wasn't convinced that he really wanted to change his lifestyle. Because work was Terry's way of defining himself, she feared that he would not slow his pace, even if his health were in jeopardy, which it was. She confessed that Terry had lost interest in her, both physically and emotionally. He didn't seem capable of having fun anymore. His sole ambition was to succeed at work and make a name for himself. She did not think he was enjoying work, but he seemed to have no other way to gain self-worth.

Fifteen minutes later Rene quit talking. She looked at me and let the emotion rise to the surface. I could see that she was very frightened about Terry's well-being and their marriage.

"What if Terry doesn't want to change?" she asked. "What if he keeps going at this pace? I don't want to be married to the distant, depressed CEO of a software company. But he won't listen to me."

Rene and I talked about depression and excessive work, two syndromes that are often related to one another. We talked about how she could help him deal with these problems and communicate to him, honestly and earnestly, what she saw and what she expected from their relationship. The three of us met together at our next session. Terry and Rene had obviously already done some talking about the situation. Terry seemed more relaxed and less rigid. We spent that hour, and several hours during the next few weeks, discussing what was driving Terry, his underlying fears and insecurities, and the impact his behaviors were having on him and his marriage. He was surprisingly willing to consider alternative behaviors. He seemed to understand that if he continued down the path he was on he would lose his health, his previously happy lifestyle, and his marriage.

During one of our early sessions I used what Dr. David Burns, in his bestselling book, *The Feeling Good Handbook,* calls the Cost-Benefit Analysis. Terry seemed to appreciate this rational approach to change.

> The cost-benefit analysis is quite different from other cognitive techniques because it deals with your negative thoughts from a perspective of motivation rather than truth. Ask yourself, "How will it help me to believe this negative thought and how will it hurt me?" If it turns out the disadvantages are greater, you will find it easier to talk back to the thought.[1]

Terry explored the powerful inner message that told him he had to please his bosses at all costs, that he had to make lots of money, that he had to work as hard, if not harder, than his colleagues. Together we explored the true cost if Terry continued working as hard as he was working. What would he stand to gain, and what would he stand to lose?

Blue-Collar Blues

I have spent the majority of my life in the Pacific Northwest. For years, work here has revolved around one thing—trees. More specifically, the logging, yarding, stacking, hauling, and milling of those trees. The life of trees and the lives of the men who risk their lives in this dangerous industry are the stuff of many books and a great deal of folklore. From early on, we read of Paul Bunyan and his mighty skill with the ax. We grow up almost revering those who have gone before, carving out lives and cities amid the lush forests.

I grew up in a forested part of the state, in a town where the major employers were Weyerhaeuser and Georgia Pacific, both behemoths in the lumber industry. I was raised close to water dotted with floating logs ready for the mill and bordered by lush green forest. For years, nearly everyone I knew was involved in the timber industry in one way or another. The woods seemed to permeate our lives.

My brother and I put ourselves through school working in the woods. We spent many weekends cutting alder poles, used in refining aluminum, and stacking them on an old International truck. We felt (and still feel) proud about having worked in the woods.

As a psychologist, I still feel a kinship with timber workers because so many of the people I counsel have ties to that industry. Logging touches our lives in ways both seen and unseen. Log trucks seem to own the highways. Logs, lumber, and the economic prosperity they provide command our respect.

When someone in a mill town comments on the smell spewing from smokestacks on the horizon, the locals respond, "That's the smell of money." Indeed, the lumber industry has created jobs for generations of workers.

But other things come with jobs at one of the local mills: hard work and erratic hours. Mill workers commonly work rotating shifts—one week of day shift, one of swing, and one of graveyard. As you can imagine, this schedule leaves the worker bleary-eyed and out of sorts. He is unable to establish any type of routine. Without the four-day weekend at the end of it all, I think many would suffer severely from exhaustion and sleep deprivation.

The mills have been extremely slow to look at the dehumanizing impact these rotating shifts have on workers and their families. For many years, I wondered why the companies could not provide saner work conditions. Recently, they have become more progressive in creating schedules that have a less detrimental impact on workers. For example, some workers don't have to change shifts so frequently. But the changes have come grudgingly, and much damage has been done.

What is the result of working years of rotating shifts?

Money

These workers—the great majority of whom are men—make lots of money! The lure of continuing the rotating shifts, even when they have an opportunity to switch to straight days, is the pay differential companies offer to those who are willing to pummel their bodies into submission. The money is good! These men, often lacking a college education, are able to make more than many people with advanced degrees.

In addition to working rotating shifts, many workers add overtime. Working a swing shift, and possibly an overtime graveyard shift, is enough of an incentive to tempt even the most reluctant worker.

The money from all this labor translates into a lifestyle that may include an extended-cab pickup, fishing boat, motor home, and lengthy vacations. People hear their coworkers talking about their toys, and the temptation is too much to resist.

Emotional Exhaustion

If only workers could make enough money to live the high life while also having the time and energy to enjoy it. Unfortunately, many workers walk around in a zombielike state of exhaustion. They even chide one another about being "the drone on graveyard." They have no time for adequate sleep, no strength to exercise properly, no energy for children and spouses. People who work this hard rarely spend time recreating—they're busy recuperating. Part of the mind is willing, but the body rebels. Enough already!

Physical Depletion

The equation is quite simple. When you work your body harder than it can handle, it will eventually break down. The body often gives out first. When stress levels remain high for a significant period, without time off to recuperate and rest, physical debilitation will result.

Unfortunately, most men refuse to complain. They are tired and cranky but will not admit to themselves or their families that they cannot work like this any longer. More often, they will continue to force themselves to work while exhausted because of the financial and social pressures to do so.

In her wonderful book *Keeping the Sabbath Wholly,* Marva Dawn discusses the importance of rest to the body. In fact, she notes God's design that we should only work so much and then pull back and rest. Genesis 2:3 says, "And God blessed the seventh day and made it holy, because on it he rested from all the work of creating that he had done."

Dawn talks about the importance of Sabbath rest as a way of saving us from becoming depleted. She recommends that we "cease not only from work itself, but also from the need to accomplish and be productive, from worry and tension that accompany our modern criterion of efficiency, from efforts to be in control of our lives as if we were God."[2]

Did you catch the importance of her last five words? "…as if we were God." Excessive work for any of us confuses the roles of God and humankind. We are not divine. We cannot continue to work. God has ordained that we must rest.

Depression

When work drains the body and overtime shifts prevent a replenishing lifestyle, the result is depression. Depression, in this sense, is a reasonable response to this set of circumstances. When our work includes unreasonable challenges to the body and mind, depression is understandable. We lose creativity. Our zest for work disappears.

Whether a mill worker working rotating shifts or a high-powered software engineer like Terry, a conscientious employee must remember that work can deplete the body of needed resources and energy. It may lead to physical exhaustion and emotional depression.

As you worry about what might be wrong with your man, you might consider how much his work life contributes to his malaise. Consider the possibility that he has neglected his physical and emotional well-being for so long that his body and mind have begun to shut down.

A Neglected Family

The effects of overtime, exhaustion, and depression are not confined to the worker. The entire family is affected.

Perhaps this is where you can relate. Perhaps you are a wife and mother, and you are watching the man you love disintegrate. Perhaps he is absent—if not physically, then emotionally. The children ask where their father is and if he will be at their next piano recital or soccer game. They feel abandoned, as do you. You ask him to quit working so hard—even if you have to make some financial sacrifices—but your words fall on deaf ears. "You don't understand," he says. "Jobs like mine are hard to come by. If I don't work the overtime, someone else will. If I don't do the job, they'll find someone else to do it." He raises the ante, and you are left speechless. Responding to such defensiveness is difficult.

Remember the value of the communication tools learned earlier in this book (the Seven C's).

Spiritual Dullness

God has created us with a mind, a will, and emotions. We are spiritual as well as physical creatures. We cannot separate one part of our self from another. When we are physically exhausted, we cannot feel complete spiritually.

In my experience, both professionally and personally, when men are tired and irritable, they are not tuned in spiritually. They lose the enthusiasm that comes from walking in step with God. Their interest in reading Scripture or attending church fades. This is often the result of neglecting our spiritual life in favor of the all-important idol of our lives—work.

Another Look at Lifestyle

Thankfully, depression is not some malady that jumps out of nowhere to bite us on the behind. It is a predictable outcome to a set of factors that we have already partially discussed. If we can predict and understand these factors, we can often interrupt and change them. This is great news. It means that depression is a problem that we can deal with.

When we engage in negative behaviors, such as excessive work, we become exhausted, give up pleasurable activities, forfeit our relationship with God, and deplete our bodies to the point of debilitation. If, in addition to these factors, we encounter additional stressors, such as significant emotional loss, we are prone to depression. Our task is to analyze what we are doing that might be excessively stressful and what we have eliminated that might restore us to good health.

Sound simple enough? Here is an exercise to help us understand the problem. You can do this yourself and encourage your man to do it as well.

Activities Analysis

When was the last time you really evaluated how you spend your time? I remember a college class where we were asked to consider that question. The professor asked us to list our favorite activities and rank their value in terms of importance. Then he told us to note next to each activity how often we had engaged in it in the past month.

While the professor carried on with his lecture, I stared at
my list. I reflected on each of the activities I rated as being pleasurable to me. I remembered the backpack trip to the Enchant-
ment Lakes in Washington with some buddies. I remembered
the kayak trip down the Kalama River with my sons (I nearly
flipped near a whirlpool, scaring myself half to death). I pic-
tured myself mountain biking in Arizona with my friend Jack
and remembered nursing my wounds after spilling headlong
into the dirt.

I was pleased at the expansive list of activities that I found
to be pleasurable. I scanned the page:

playing basketball	watching funny videos
playing tennis	kayaking
sailing	journal writing
snowshoeing	yoga
backpacking	dancing
soaking in a hot tub	listening to music
bicycling	jogging
attending educational retreats	visiting bookstores
writing letters	

As I examined the list and noted how infrequently I had
engaged in these activities, my delight quickly turned to discouragement. I was shocked by my responses. I had not taken
my bicycle out of the garage for six weeks. What had happened
to the guys' annual summer backpacking adventure that we
had vowed to continue as long as our legs and backs could
handle the challenge? My journaling had slipped into a once-
a-week affair, even though I am aware that daily writing keeps

my emotions on an even keel. And what about my boat? I love sailing, yet I hadn't been out on the water for weeks. I hadn't even been by to turn over the engine, a part of routine maintenance.

The professor kept lecturing, a distant voice in the background, while I engaged in self-examination. Why hadn't I taken out my boat or spent time with friends in so long? The question demanded an answer, yet I did not want to be honest. I feared that honesty would make me feel even worse. Maybe I wasn't ready to confront the question and finger the culprit.

Work!

I was working more and allowing my business and busyness to crowd out the joys of life. I was suffering from what Charles Hummel called "the tyranny of the urgent." All of the urgent things of life, the supposed necessary responsibilities, were crowding out the pleasures.

I tuned back in to the professor for the next assignment. "What have you noticed on your sheet of paper? Are you spending your time the way you want to spend your time, or does something need to change?"

This was a no-brainer. As I looked around the room, others appeared to experience similar epiphanies. What were we doing with this one, precious life God had given us? Did we want our families and friends to know us as people who gave it all to their work? Did we want to forfeit those activities that brought joy to our lives?

Now it's your turn. Take a moment and make a list of your favorite, replenishing activities. How often are you doing them? What do you need to add, limit, or eliminate from your life? What steps can take you in the right direction?

Losing Our Soul at Work

If, in the first several chapters of this book, you have seen things that fit you and your man, then he needs you now more than ever before. Why? Because the situation is not likely to get better without your help! Let's look more closely at what is happening and what needs to happen to reclaim lost ground.

When men leave it all at work, they are leaving more than just their physical energies. Yes, they need rest and replenishment and a shift of focus. But we must also talk about the spiritual realm and how it suffers from an obsession with work.

How are we to know if we have lost something deeper than simple physical energy at the mill or the office? Lee Bolman and Terrence Deal, in their book *Leading with Soul*, say a loss of spirit occurs in many men and women today.

> Its symptoms are loss of seriousness, enthusiasm, and zest. When individuals live superficially, pursue no goals deeper than material success, and never stop to listen to their inner voices, they block their spiritual development....Today's stressful and turbulent world compounds the risk of stunted souls and spiritual malaise.[3]

Perhaps you know the feeling or can recognize these symptoms in your man:

- a loss of vitality
- a loss of enthusiasm
- a loss of creativity
- a loss of excitement about work

These are indicators that you or your man have lost heart at work. They represent a cry from the soul for something more meaningful, something that reignites the passions.

Work as Calling

Work is nearly always more than work, and that can be a good thing. A job that is just a job is a futile thing. It leads to a loss of spirit because we have no stake in it, and it provides us with no sense of fulfillment. Thankfully, spirit can be recaptured. For you or your man to recapture lost spirit, you must be willing to come alive again. You must open your senses to what is going on. If you are work-weary, this may be difficult to do. But you can make a start. One day you will see something, feel something, or hear something new that will touch you deeply.

For many, an epiphany comes as a gentle nudge, such as a desire to take an interesting class at your local college. It may come as a small desire to sing in the church choir or perhaps read a book that has received good reviews. It may come in the form of envy—someone else's lifestyle or job looks interesting. Follow the nudge to see where it leads. Why does the grass look greener, and what is your fascination with it? This can be a beginning.

David Whyte, author of *Crossing the Unknown Sea: Work as a Pilgrimage of Identity*, shares his agony as an executive who kept feeling "called" to be a poet. This particular pull was, of course, foreign to a man enmeshed in the business world. How could he give up a lucrative career to follow his calling to something as obscure and financially limiting as poetry?

As for most of us, his journey is circuitous. Rarely does anyone find a direct, laser-quick path to his or her true calling. It's not that easy. Whyte tells of feeling "lost" in his work—a condition he wrestled with for some time. He had "disappeared under a swampy morass of stress and speed....I had become a stranger to myself....I obviously had a violent need to find myself and give myself a good talking-to."

Relief for Whyte came when he drank a glass of red wine with his friend Brother David, a monk, in a cottage by the sea. Brother David loved poetry with a similar passion.

Whyte finally mustered the courage to ask the question that had been haunting him.

> "Tell me of exhaustion," I said.
>
> He looked at me with an acute, searching, compassionate ferocity for the briefest of moments, as if trying to sum up the entirety of the situation and without missing a beat, as if he had been waiting all along, to say a life-changing thing to me. He said, in the form both of a question and an assertion:
>
> "You know the antidote to exhaustion is not necessarily rest?"
>
> "The antidote to exhaustion is not necessarily rest," I repeated woodenly, as if I might exhaust myself completely before I reached the end of the sentence. "What is it, then?"
>
> "The antidote to exhaustion is wholeheartedness.... You are like Rilke's Swan in his awkward waddling across the ground; the swan doesn't cure his awkwardness by beating himself on the back, by moving faster, or by trying to organize himself better. He does it by moving toward the elemental water,

where he belongs. It is the simple contact with the water that gives him grace and presence. You only have to touch the elemental waters in your own life, and it will transform everything. But you have to let yourself down into those waters from the ground on which you stand, and that can be hard. Particularly if you think you might drown."[4]

The point of the story is that we must listen to our hearts, listen to our unique callings. When we cling to old, unhealthy ways of living and working as if they were the only right possibilities, we die. To put it another way, we must listen to the movement of the Spirit in our lives to give us new breath, new energy. In order to do that, we must be willing to give up what we have known for so long and trust that God knows what He is doing in our lives.

We can trust that God has a unique and empowering calling for each of us. Listen to the Bible's first five words: "In the beginning God created..." (Genesis 1:1). God fashioned a universe out of nothing. He created us in His image. We too have creative energies that He expects us to use. When we abandon our creative energies, when we give up our individuality to the corporate vision, we no longer work from our hearts. We begin using our will to force things, and work becomes a *job* that is little more than an obligation. This is not what the Creator intended when He fashioned us.

What is your calling? What are your unique gifts? When you think of your man, consider whether he has strayed from his passions. What has been the result, and how can you help him refocus? Can he go out on a limb and pursue some new interest while still paying the bills? It's possible.

Helping Your Man Find His Calling

Has your man sold his soul to the company? Has he lost his enthusiasm for work, or perhaps done the opposite—given his heart and soul to work, leaving precious little room for you and the family? If so, don't give up hope. You may be the one who can help him. Consider a few possibilities:

First, you know your man better than anyone else does, perhaps even better than he knows himself. You are in a unique position to offer him feedback on his spiritual gifts and passions. You know what is stirring in his heart and what he may have left behind in his corporate climbing. You are able to see what excites him and what he would love to be doing with his life. Remind him.

Second, consider for a moment how you might affirm his calling—that is, offer him support for the spiritual and emotional pull coming from a particular direction. Consider offering him your reflections on his life, just as you might offer direction to your children as they are growing and changing. Point out the strengths that you see latent within him, or recite back to him what you have been hearing him say for some time about his passions. Tell him that he deserves the right to pursue his creative yearnings. This kind of affirmation is sometimes enough to move a person to make a decision.

Third, help create an environment where he can test out his ideas, a place where he can be safe in voicing his doubts and fears. You know that no move toward creativity ever happened without resistance and fear. Allow him a "sanctuary" where he can talk about his mixed feelings.

Fourth, brainstorm with him about possible ways for him to follow the path that offers him happiness. Perhaps this will simply mean changing something at his current job so that he has more creative possibilities. It may mean going back to school so that he can learn a new trade. It might mean finding a way to start another career part-time while he lets go of his current job. You can help him find the answers he needs to move forward.

For many, change will not be drastic. It will be fine-tuning a life that has come out of tune. It may mean keeping his current job while altering his lifestyle to include the pursuits and interests that added zing to your life and his. It may mean agreeing, as a family, to do without some things so that he does not have to work overtime.

Rene and Terry successfully changed their lives. He made some difficult decisions to cut back at work and to invest more time and energy into his marriage and personal life. His marriage, as well as his physical and spiritual health, have improved. He and Rene have made a pact to help one another keep their lives balanced. He has regained genuine enthusiasm for his work, but he is trying to keep it all in perspective. Work is never supposed to preoccupy one's life.

You have a wonderful opportunity to be an inspirational force for him and for yourself as well. You understand that any calling upon our lives involves risk. In order to move forward, you both will need to stare down that risk and take chances. Julia Cameron, in her book *The Artist's Way at Work,* said it well. "Ambition that arises from your authentic self is different from the mere lust for money and power as ends unto themselves. True ambition understands that no one lives forever. In claiming your ambition, you dedicate yourself to a quest."[5]

As you explore possibilities and prayerfully listen to the stirrings of your heart, I trust that you will be courageous on your journey. Courage will serve you well.

chapter 6

No Buddy's Home: Friendships

On my father's wedding day, no one was there to hold him.
Noble loneliness held him. Since he never asked for pity his
friends thought he was whole. Walking alone, he could carry it.
　　　　　　　—ROBERT BLY, "MY FATHER'S WEDDING, 1924"

AT THIS WRITING, WE HAVE JUST ENDURED one of the biggest winter storms in recent Pacific Northwest history. Not that it compared in any way to the blasts that regularly hit the Midwest or New England states, but for us, it was big. The temperature fell to a numbing ten degrees, and pipes burst with regularity, keeping plumbers busy around the clock. The skies dumped several inches of snow, snapping electrical lines and snarling traffic. Activity came to a complete halt in cities and suburbs where streets were impassable to all but the stoutest four-wheel drives.

With the new weather technology available to meteorologists, we knew about the storm in advance—just long enough to create an atmosphere of panic, excitement, and frenzy. The forecast did little to help us navigate safely, with cars spinning like ice cubes on a Formica counter, but at home most of us were prepared. We had lined up to grab generators and foodstuffs as if another world war were about to take place. We chopped wood, bought candles, and made sure we had extra batteries for our flashlights. News teams delighted in giving us round-the-clock coverage.

We will remember the storm of '04 for years to come, but it is still not the biggest news for men in this part of the country. It hit hard but was over quickly.

The weather is not what dominates men's minds this time of year. This is January, after all, and January can only mean one thing: the early rounds of the pro football playoffs leading up to the granddaddy of all sports events, the Super Bowl.

Sports radio programs are replete with second-guessing as the pundits discuss who is favored and why. Will the Patriots go all the way, or will they be stopped on the path to the big game? What about the Carolina Panthers or the Philadelphia Eagles? All this talk serves as fodder for men to show off their knowledge of the game and to engage in friendly banter. On my commute home, I listen to callers ask radio talk-show hosts questions about statistical minutia concerning players and their performance, and make predictions about the playoffs. Football occupies men's (and women's) minds through the chilly winter months. It provides a way for men to connect with one another, albeit superficially.

Unfortunately, too often the connection stops there—with friendly banter. All of this talk is not really what men need.

If men do not need a sports roundtable, another golf buddy, or a gym rat friend to spot them as they strain to press more weight, what do they need? What could be missing? That is the thousand-dollar question and one that you, as helpmate to your man, may also wonder about.

Men do not need more adrenaline-producing sporting events or strategies that will help them become successful in the business world. Men don't need more ways to compete with one another. In fact, they need quite the opposite. We must find ways to get beyond the superficiality and truly connect with one another. And that is a tall order for men. For all of our loneliness and depression, we need connection. Real connection.

Jousting at Windmills

As you observe the behavior of men, you may be reminded of Don Quixote, the lead character in the novel of the same name by Miguel de Cervantes. In this fascinating read, which is required by many high school English teachers, Don Quixote is a gaunt, gangly, middle-aged man who fashions himself to be a knight. Having read too many books about chivalrous heroes, he sets out to win the honor of his invented love, Dulcinea. Like most men, he longs for a sense of purpose.

Unfortunately, Don Quixote seems to confuse fantasy and reality at times. The reader is left wondering whether or not Don Quixote is mad, confused, or a little of both. He is able to speak lucidly about literature and other topics, yet at the same time, he jousts at windmills as if they were attacking knights.

From a distance, men may appear to be quixotic. They may appear to be slightly out of touch with reality—dashing about in pursuit of the elusive dollar, much to the chagrin of their mates, pummeling their bodies into submission in an attempt to gain the admiration of others, carousing at local bars in an effort to silence the pain and sadness of feeling disconnected from others. They seem to spend their lives frantically producing something, anything, in order to prove they have a purpose. They believe this is the only way to deal with the gnawing emptiness within.

Either Don Quixote is mad or he is able to convince the reader that he is in a world of his own making. He is surrounded by people, yet he remains tragically alone.

The story captures our curiosity. Could it be because we know of many men who are chasing windmills of their own, caught up in foolish pursuits that have no real meaning? Their "quest" may be a bit more grounded but still involve chasing something unattainable. In the end, they are discouraged and detached from others.

You may feel a need to reach into your man's "Don Quixote world" and shake him. Like Quixote's faithful companion, Sancho Panza, you may want to talk him into seeing the truth about whatever matter he is dealing with.

You want to tell him that the inns he sees as castles are just inns. Dulcinea is a figment of his imagination. You want to help him work out of his blues, and you rightly believe that being honest about his plight is the place to begin. Let's talk about ways to help him get back on the right path.

Superficial Relationships

Many men are, like Quixote, foolish, if not deluded. We seek relief from ailments we know little about. We want real connection with others but are inept at creating that connection in our lives. Thus, we sometimes appear to be flailing at windmills and trying to bring honor to imaginary Dulcineas. We want to be connected to others, to have real relationships, but we dare not ask the price. Even worse, we usually won't even ask directions.

Men are not great at connecting on a deep level. Most men seem content to get together with their buddies occasionally to hunt, fish, play a game of handball, watch football, or drink beer. Seldom do we stop to consider that these activities miss the mark. Even men's Bible study groups leave most men wanting. Why is that?

In their book *The Wild Man's Journey,* Richard Rohr and Joseph Martos provide us with a clue:

> Our technological society, and especially our business world, does not give men any encouragement for the inner journey of self-discovery and spiritual development. In fact, just the opposite. If you are a business executive or in business for yourself, you have to spend so much time keeping up and trying to get ahead that you often don't have time for relationships with others, much less for a relationship with yourself or God....
>
> By and large, the Church is no help, either. The western world has turned the Church into another corporation, with corporate headquarters downtown in the bishop's office and with company stores conveniently located all around the city and suburbs...The gospel, however, is not at all concerned about the organization of the Church. It is concerned with conversion and transformation, both of the individual and of society itself....
>
> How can you organize the spiritual journey? You can't. How can you organize self-transformation and conversion? It's impossible.[1]

And so, many men are left wandering around without a map to guide them on their inner journey of emotional and spiritual development. They are drifting, and at some level they know it. As their partners, you know it too.

The common complaint I hear repeatedly from women is that their relationships lack depth. Women want a man who

pays attention to them and to their relationship. They want a
man who reflects on his actions. They want a man with depth
and with the ability to be a partner in a mature and fully sat-
isfying relationship.

If this is to occur, it must start with his ability to develop
deep friendships.

Father Hunger

To encourage a man to relate on a deeper level, we must
first look at some of the barriers to this inner journey. Without
question, to invite a man to travel the path to deeper emotional
and spiritual understanding is to ask him to be very courageous.

We must consider an important topic for both men and
women—the issue of "father hunger," or "the father wound"
as some have labeled it. This is at the root of many men's difficulties, especially their ability to relate to one another. It is a central barrier to their willingness to embark on the inner journey.

Again, I refer to the seminal work of Rohr and Martos. They
suggest that most men have not dealt with a wound that their
fathers inflicted. Most men have a father wound because their
father was absent due to death or divorce or because the father's
work kept him away from home much of the time. Too often,
even when a father is present, he is aloof from his children and
his wife.

The result of this distance is a deep hurt, "a deprivation that
leads to a poor sense of one's own center and boundaries, a
mind that is disconnected from one's body and emotions, and
the passivity of an unlit fire."[2]

A refusal to engage the inner wound also alienates men from
one another. Rohr and Martos explain.

Not having reached the deep masculine within them, they look to other men for assurance and affirmation. Not having found that inner strength, which gives them a sense of their own personal stability, they are constantly trying to prove who they are. Whether they engage in *macho* games of physical fitness, sexual prowess or business success, they are trying to show themselves and others that they have made it, that they are really men. But their continuous running from one accomplishment to another only proves that they have not made it and subconsciously they feel their own incompleteness. Not having found their self-worth, they try to prove their value by making money, accumulating the things money can buy and exercising power. But their constant search for earner worth, in fact, betrays their inner sense of worthlessness.[3]

Jacob came to see me a few months ago. This tall, tanned, and slender man has been married for seven years to his wife, Gail. He is an accomplished dentist and astute businessman. In his mid thirties, he has achieved much in his few short years in the profession. He is on the board of the Chamber of Commerce, holds a leadership position at the local Rotary Club, serves as an elder on his church board, and has a thriving practice that I am sure earns him a healthy six-figure income. He is on the unofficial Who's Who list of rising stars in the community. He is a mover and shaker.

Jacob told me that he has read nearly every book he could find on optimal performance. He said that he wants to be able to retire at age 40, if he so desires. He has begun acquiring apartment buildings that he renovates and then rents. He has taken courses on how to maximize his business by ensuring that most of his patients are "top-end" and can afford his high-priced line of cosmetic dentistry. He sees nearly everything he does as a networking opportunity, a way to make even more money. He is clearly on a path to success—at least in one area of his life.

Jacob was cautious but deliberate about contacting me for an appointment. He has, through much reading, developed a "mind over matter" philosophy that leaves little room for failure, self-doubt, or psychologists. Yet, he is also a practical man. "I know when it is time to reach out for a little help," he said. "I want to know what you think about a few things."

I learned that, despite all of his success, he still has some nagging doubts about his profession and his personal life. He had tried to wall these doubts off from his consciousness, but they kept returning.

Jacob shared how he had grown tired of the tedium of dentistry. His practice had grown; he now worked six days a week, partly because he needed to pay for the new office complex he built the year before. He did good work, and his reputation had spread throughout the community. Subsequently, the referrals poured in. This, Jacob said, was both a blessing and a curse. While he wanted to be in demand and had grown accustomed to the nice income, he had been forced to give up the lifestyle he had dreamed about. I asked Jacob to tell me about that.

"Ten years ago I imagined that I would be situated in a nice office in a small town much like this one. I would work four days a week and then take a day off to do some sailing. I wanted to reserve weekends exclusively for my daughters and wife. I wanted to feel connected to my church—not just fill a function there. I wanted to live that "nice house with a white picket fence" dream. But something happened along the way. I got the bug to make a lot of dollars and started hanging around with other high achievers. I found out I could make a bunch of money, serve on prestigious boards, and have a lot of influence in the community, which is kind of nice. But I think I'm giving up my dreams along the way."

"Tell me about your friendships and family," I said.

"My friendships have always been very important to me. In college, the guys and I had a blast. I was out sailing with them at least once a week. Sailing was great because it gave us a chance to really talk about things—about life, relationships, money, family, God...I really connected to that group of guys. They were all willing to talk openly about the deeper things in life. Sometimes we weren't really out there to sail—we wanted to catch up on each other's lives and share our own. Sailing was conducive to that.

"I remember one friend—Cade. I hear from him every so often, but in those days we were very close. He was a short, pudgy guy with big, Coke-bottle glasses. He was a lit major and would bring poetry that I found myself enjoying. He would read John Donne and e. e. cummings to us. He brought tapes of Rod McKuen that we would listen to. We spent hours talking about what the authors were saying. Cade was a thinker. He would sit in the cockpit and let the rest of us manage the sails while he served up the poetry *du jour*. We talked about our parents, our relationships with our dads, and everything else we could think of. But now— "

Jacob appeared sad and discouraged about losing contact with his friends. He clearly missed those gatherings with other men—the sailing and talking, the time that was open and free and available for reflection and wonder. He now longed for spaces in the day when he could simply let his imagination run free.

"I can relate, Jacob. I'm a sailor too. I always take a good book to discuss with friends. I've never wanted to just sail, as much fun as that is. Like you, I want to talk about the deeper things in life. I want to really connect with guys I can trust. There is something powerful about men talking straight with other men."

"I thought that would continue after dental school, but it hasn't," Jacob said. "I've focused on building the practice and being involved in the community. Somehow I let my friendships slide, and I don't like where it's left me. I stopped hanging out with friends and doing my guy stuff. I'm so focused on work that there is no room for friendships."

"Why do you think this has happened, Jacob?"

"My dad is a dentist, too. Growing up, he was never home. I told myself that I didn't want to be as busy as he was. But now I am.

"Dad pushed me to excel at everything I did. Like I said, he was gone a lot when I was a kid. I always wondered why he never came to my baseball games. Now I know. He was busy doing the things I'm doing now. He was on the school board for years, spending every spare minute building his practice and trying to be everything to everybody. I guess I figured the only way to get close to him was to try to impress him. He gets excited when I talk to him now about the practice or tell him about a big financial investment I've made. I wonder if I'm trying too hard to gain his approval."

Jacob went on to tell me that he rarely found time to sit and talk with other men anymore. He worked out at the gym but found his encounters there to be shallow and unfulfilling.

He did serve on the elder board at his church and found that time to be somewhat purposeful. But, he said, in the end it felt like just another obligation. At times, he felt used by the pastor. Jacob was one of a group of wealthy professionals who were running the church like a business and not really connecting to the needs of the members.

Even amid the flurry of his many activities, Jacob felt lonely and discontented.

Jacob's malaise and depression were obvious. He was overworked and undernourished emotionally, relationally, and spiritually. In a few short years, he had done what countless other men have done:

- bought into society's definition of success
- got caught up in accumulating more and more
- started working harder and harder for more and more hours
- left his buddies and real friendships behind
- abandoned his wife and children in pursuit of material success
- lost sight of his spiritual goals

Jacob's situation is common today. Men are working harder than ever, trying to find something in their careers that just isn't there. Actually, they are still searching for something from their fathers.

Fathers have unwittingly added to the estrangement of men from other men. Though they are not solely responsible, fathers play an instrumental role in determining how men develop and what drives them. In a book titled *The Rag and Bone Shop of the Heart*, editors Robert Bly, James Hillman, and Michael Meade note the uncertainties of the child's relationship to the father.

> The father may be in question himself: Where is he? Is the father here? Who is the father, is the father known? Whether in the hands waiting or long gone, the father inevitably brings distance to the child's

world. And sadness. He is somewhere beyond the
falling, reaching, calling of the child.[4]

This struggle is further illustrated in a poem about fathers
and sons, in the same book:

> For brother, what are we?
> We are sons of our father,
> Whose face we have never seen,
> We are the sons of the father,
> Whose voice we have never heard,
> We are the sons of our father,
> To whom we have cried for strength and comfort
> In our agony,
> We are the sons of our father,
> Whose life like ours
> Was lived in solitude and in the wilderness,
> We are the sons of our father,
> To whom only can we speak out
> The strange, dark burden of our heart and spirit,
> We are the sons of our father,
> And we shall follow the print of his foot forever.[5]
>
> —Thomas Wolfe

An Empty Soul

Another way to talk about the barrier that father hunger
creates for men is to talk about the hole in the soul that so many
men feel. Men often have an empty place inside that they are
incessantly trying to fill—in any way possible. We don't think
about it much, but it is always there. Call it father hunger. Call
it a need for other men to admire and affirm us. We have a need
that women cannot fill, no matter how hard they try.

This notion, that men need men, is often perplexing to women. They often feel, unnecessarily, that they cannot be enough for men. The truth is, women could never be enough for men. Men have been designed by God to need other men to achieve a healthy balance in their lives. Just as women need female friendships, and men cannot take their place, so too men need male friendships. Frank Pittman addresses this in his book *Man Enough:*

> Life for most boys and for many grown men is a frustrating search for the lost father who has not yet offered protection, provision, nurturing, modeling, or especially, anointment.... They go through their puberty rituals day after day for a lifetime, waiting for a father to anoint them and say, "Attaboy," to treat them as good enough to be considered a man.... They call attention to their pain, getting into trouble, getting hurt, doing things that are bad for them, as if they are calling for a father to come take them in hand and straighten them out, or at least tell them how a grown man would handle the pain....
>
> [Boys] compete with other boys, but they don't let the other boys see their shame over not feeling like men, over not having been anointed, and so they don't know that the other boys feel the same....[6]

Boys who would be men must leave the company of women. If they're lucky, they'll have fathers and mentors to model masculinity for them, to nurture them through the tests of manhood, and to anoint them when they are man enough; they'll have heroes to inspire them and point the way; and they'll have companions on the path to manhood. One's buddies

may be the most encouraging voices in any man's male
chorus, or they may be the most rigid and demanding.
But without those voices, masculinity is lonely indeed.[7]

I have done a great deal of work on issues surrounding my
relationships with my father and with my sons. I have long been
a believer that men need other men to truly heal from the father
wound. To this end, I have participated in hours of men's group
sessions. I have expressed anger toward my father for working
too hard during my youth. I have shared with him my frustration that he was not available to me when I needed his admiration and approval. We have cried together and healed those
wounds.

Part of my healing has come from work I have done as a
father. I have asked forgiveness from my sons for being absent
during some of their formative experiences. The sins of the
father seem to be passed down through generations, and I have
spent countless hours recovering from workaholism. I have
been intentional about playing an active role in my sons' lives
since an epiphany I received when they were eight and ten years
old. I decided then that I would no longer work so hard if
doing so meant missing so much of their lives. It was a slow
road back into their lives after being "gone" so long. Thankfully, they have responded favorably to my journey back to
them.

My healing has not stopped. I have been blessed with a father
who still wants to be a part of my life and makes time for me.
I have also been blessed with sons who want to share their lives
with me. We continue to heal and move forward together.

My personal and professional work has convinced me of one
thing—men have a hole in their souls that must be healed.

Establishing meaningful relationships with fathers, sons, and friends is a pretty good place to start.

Homophobia

In our struggle to allow ourselves to get close to other men, we have a huge barrier to overcome. Pittman talks candidly about the challenge of homophobia, something all men wonder about, deny, and struggle with more than they would like to admit.

> The greatest threat boys and men feel to their sense of themselves as men is their fear that they, or someone else, will find "homosexuality" inside them. Whatever homosexuality is or isn't, the fear of it is crippling and painfully isolating.... Our confused, panicky, and scientifically invalid theories about homosexuality create awful problems both for the men who live a homosexual life and for the great majority of us who live a heterosexual life. Most straight men, whether or not they went through the typical adolescent confusion and anxiety about their sexual identity, live in fear of finding homosexuality in themselves or catching it, and so they don't get close to one another as they desperately need to get.[8]

As if men don't already have enough barriers to connecting with other men, here is yet one more wall that they must scale. For some, it is a sheer cliff without a single toehold. Others may have gained enough comfort with their sexuality that they do not feel a need to avoid closeness with other men. They also do not feel a need to prove their masculinity to others.

Homophobia is something that all men must address, if not in a group, at least within the sanctuary of their minds. If they don't, it can pose a formidable barrier to forming friendships with other men.

Lacking Respect

Men first come to my therapy group because they must. They often return, after their time is up, because they found something they didn't know they needed—respect from other men and from me.

Lack of respect for others is a huge obstacle to true connection. I make no bones about the fact that I respect the men who come to my office. But too often they do not respect each other. Not really. These are men whom society has labeled criminals, and so they are. These are men who are despised for hurting women. Yet I find in them something I find in all men: a vulnerable inner self that craves attention and love.

At first, the men posture with each other. They like to joke about what they did last Friday night. They strut their stuff, puffing themselves up in that primitive behavior designed to make them look good. But they eventually realize they only look foolish.

"Who are you trying to kid?" one man will ask another. "Remember who you are talking to here." In the group setting, men receive permission to relinquish childish antics and get down to the real work of being honest about where they hurt. When they move beyond the superficialities, they can heal. Here they are truly men. True manhood and maturity come from sharing what really makes them happy or sad. By uncovering their vulnerability, they allow other men to get close. Once they have moved beyond the homophobic fears and paranoia, they can find safety in the gathering of men, and healing can begin. And it does.

Being this vulnerable with each other naturally leads to spiritual things. I am comfortable in sharing my faith, and that honest sharing seems to naturally lead the men to talk about spiritual matters. We are able to work to an admission: We don't have the answers, and God does. This humility is a wonderful beginning for these men as they try to reassemble their lives.

Women Are Relational

If men need a gathering of men and brotherly friendship to heal, what role can women play? Where is the balance between the need for men to rely on one another and the need for women to support men on their journey? How can women assist men to find deep healing and develop friendships? Fortunately, women can play a pivotal role in creating social opportunities for men.

Men need to take advantage of the opportunities that exist to develop friendships. Here are a few ideas to consider.

First, *thankfully, women are very relational.* Women's relational strengths can be an added bonus for men. Men need to watch and learn from women's relational skills. Women are naturally more social and outgoing than men. They gather together, trust one another, and know how to create a network of support. Men can learn a lot by watching and emulating women and their friendships.

Second, *women make friendships naturally.* Creating a circle of friends is challenging for men, but women often already have them established. Many women have long-established friendships that could, with a bit of work, open up opportunities for their man as well. In such cases, the work has already been done for them. They have but to reach out and take hold of the network of friends that is there.

For example, rather than going solo on your weekly lunch date with your best friends, consider inviting the men to join you. Perhaps instead of always exercising with girls only, consider inviting the men. You can casually introduce your man into your existing circle of friends in many ways. This may create opportunities for your friends to include their men in the activities as well.

Third, *women and men can naturally develop friendships together.* Couples have many opportunities, especially through church and other social gatherings, to forge friendships. Creating friendships together takes some of the pressure off men to go out and find their own friends. Consider your weekly extracurricular activities and determine which ones could include your man. This is where a book club, investment group, or business network can provide fun ways to do things together, increasing your man's social circle.

Fourth, *women need to encourage men to participate in groups that take vulnerability to a deeper level.* Churches have established "sharing groups" that offer opportunities for men to deal with personal problems and share friendship within a spiritual framework. You will need to give up some personal time with him in exchange for his participation in these growth experiences. However, the investment will pay off in the long run.

Finally, *women need to offer their support for and critical feedback about male friendships.* Women should encourage men to have healthy male friendships. Notice that I used the word "healthy" to describe positive male friendships—everything from mountain biking to meeting for coffee with friends.

Obviously, men won't gain anything by maintaining unhelpful friendships with other men.

As men attempt to leave addictions and problem behavior in their past, they will be tempted to hang on to vestiges of the old life. This can, unfortunately, take the form of old, unhealthy friendships. As a helpmate, you will sometimes need to tell your man things he does not want to hear. Yet he needs to hear them, and you are in a unique position to say them. A word of caution is in order, however—you must share your feelings from a position of love, not one of jealousy.

Jonathan and David

Perhaps the most celebrated and poignant friendship in Scripture is Jonathan and David's. Their friendship was borne of tragedy. David was an officer in King Saul's army. After proving his military prowess, David advanced through the ranks. He later married Saul's daughter and developed a close friendship with Saul's oldest son, Jonathan.

In many ways it was an unlikely relationship. Jonathan was, after all, the son of the king of Israel, Saul, who was soon to be David's adversary. Saul perceived David as a threat, and Jonathan was in the precarious position of choosing loyalties.

But we discover that David and Jonathan had several qualities necessary for an enduring, healthy friendship. Saul hand-picked David to be a general in his army, but Saul soon realized that David could be a threat to his rule. In the account of their friendship, we see that Jonathan chose to remain loyal to David in spite of his father's attempts to kill David. When Jonathan warned David of his father's intentions, we read of their emotional encounter.

> David got up from the south side of the stone and
> bowed down before Jonathan three times, with his face
> to the ground. Then they kissed each other and wept
> together—but David wept the most. Jonathan said to
> David, "Go in peace, for we have sworn friendship
> with each other in the name of the LORD" (1 Samuel
> 20:41-42).

Several qualities made the friendship of David and Jonathan
especially strong. Even in the midst of war and family strife,
their friendship contained these characteristics:

- honesty
- loyalty
- emotional support
- selfless love

At a time of despair and depression, we see David buoyed
by Jonathan's deep friendship and brotherly love. What a
wonderful model for men in the throes of personal struggle.
This biblical example shows two men who dared to offer friendship and love for one another even when doing so meant risking
death.

Men still need this kind of friendship today. All men, and
especially those struggling with the blues, need a buddy, one
who can understand how tough being a man in today's world
can be.

And men need women who understand that men need
other men. As important as intimacy with women is, it cannot
take the unique place of the friendship of other men.

Lost in the Woods: Midlife Crisis

If a plant cannot live according to its nature, it dies; and so a man.

—HENRY DAVID THOREAU

A MAN IS SUPPOSED TO KNOW MANY THINGS—how to fix things, how to be strong in the face of trouble, how to fight, how to find the answer, and definitely, how to find his way. Being lost is unmanly. The common joke is that a man must never stop and ask for directions. Although this is a joke, it contains more than a kernel of truth.

In light of this, you can understand why seeking help from a psychologist is so hard for a man.

As I greet my first client of the morning, I can see that, like me, he is not fully awake. I grab a cup of coffee, hoping the caffeine will get my brain working. He slurps his latte, and I tell myself that we are both having trouble getting started.

Ben appears to be middle-aged, perhaps 55. He wears jeans and a sport shirt. The shirt is crisply pressed, suggesting that he may be a professional. The graying beard adds a couple of years to his appearance. Perhaps he isn't as old as I initially thought.

Ben is a new client, and I begin to wonder what brought him here. I whisper a short prayer, asking God for guidance and discernment. *What are his concerns? Can I give him what he might need this morning?*

In the past few weeks, several men and women have come to me in the middle of transitions that drastically altered their lives. Would Ben be another?

He pauses now, looking up at me with a hint of moistness in his eyes—my first sign that we will be talking about something momentous. He tries to speak, but stops to clear his throat. The tears come more easily now, and he seems disinterested in stopping them.

"Why don't you tell me what's happening in your life, Ben?" I say.

"My wife just told me that she's in love with another man and is not sure she wants to stay with me. We've been married for 35 years."

I share his shock. How can this be, I wonder? After so many years. I do some quick math in my head. Thirty-five years? If he were 55, that would make him 20 when he got married.

"Tell me more about it, Ben," I say, trying to digest the magnitude of the moment. I was sitting with a man who had lived the majority of his life with this woman, and now, out of the blue, she announces that she is in love with another man. No wonder he was distraught.

"She's not sure she wants to leave. But she's obviously leaning in that direction. Our kids are mad at her, but she says she hasn't been happy for many years. I didn't know that. I'm not sure I believe it now. Why didn't she tell me? Maybe I could have done something."

I could easily believe every word. According to Ben's account, he is the victim. His wife did not tell him of her unhappiness and now, years later, she announces that she is considering a life that does not include him. He didn't know what was going on, so we cannot hold him responsible for what is happening to him.

That would be the easy interpretation. She is bad, he is good. She is a philanderer, he is the stable, loving husband and father. But there is probably more to the picture, and I remind myself to suspend judgments until I have heard the entire story—at least his version of it.

Ben continues.

His wife has told him she is thinking about moving across the country to be with her high school sweetheart, whom, she says, she has never forgotten. They have been in touch by phone, though she won't commit to how often. She says there is little reason to hope for a positive outcome. She has been trying to tell Ben for years that he is too withdrawn, too quiet, too boring, and that she is no longer interested in him. As if to reassure him, she says that he is not a bad guy. The problem is that he has had symptoms of depression he has refused to treat. He is not affectionate, he has not invested time and energy in their sexual relationship, and she wants more. She has not found friendship in their marriage for some time. She sees an opportunity and is nearly certain that she will take it.

Many readers will probably rally to my client's defense. How could she do such a thing? She would seem to be forfeiting a life of leisurely retirement, enjoyment with their grandchildren, and the history she and Ben share. But is there more to the story?

Ben sits in front of me, stunned. He has been hit with a bullet to the brain. He thought everything was going fine. Now he wonders what signals he missed. He wonders if it is too late to fix what is obviously broken. He is stumbling around, lost in the woods, with no trail to lead him back to safety. He does not remember ever feeling as lost as he does today.

He pleads with me to help him. Here he is, mid stream, with water swirling about him, ready to sweep him away. Assurances that things will be all right will do little to assuage his pain.

Understandably, Ben has not been able to sleep the past several days. His appetite is gone, and he is beginning to lose weight. He has no interest in anything except saving his marriage. He knows the outlook is not good. He must face this fact and determine how he will move on with his life if his wife is not willing to work on their marriage.

Lost in Midlife

The timing of this tragedy is no coincidence. While it certainly could have happened earlier, a high percentage of men seek help at this stage in life. Why? Because it is a natural time of transition and reflection. It is a time when many forces come together to challenge men and women individually and as couples. It is, in short, a time of instability.

When we look into Ben's life, we are tempted to focus on the recent events that brought him to my office. However, he's said that his wife has been sending messages for some time that urged him to closely examine his life and their relationship. She told him he is no fun to be around, that his enthusiasm for life has waned. She warned him numerous times that the day of reckoning would come. But he refused to believe it. He hid, dodged, worked, and denied that she would ever come to this kind of decision. Now he sits in front of me, forlorn, rejected, lost. He cannot see clearly how he got here, and he has no idea how to find his way back. He, like many men, is even more lost than he would like to admit. Let's see if we can retrace the steps that led him to where he is.

First, *he denied his depression for a long time.* His wife had been telling him that he needed to deal with it. He tried to ignore the problem, hoping it would go away and she would quit nagging him about it. He lived in a fantasy world, believing that if he stayed busy he would not have to face his problems with the blues. Unfortunately, he gambled and lost.

Second, *he and his wife failed to communicate effectively about their problems.* We dare not lay all of the responsibility for the marriage problems at Ben's feet. We do not know exactly how responsible each is for the problem. What we do know is that they failed, as a couple, to navigate the bridge of isolation that she felt. And in that isolation she looked in another direction for companionship.

Third, *he has not dealt with his responsibility to be an interesting and enlivening partner to his wife.* We do not need to lay all of the blame on Ben, but he is responsible for bringing enthusiasm into their marriage. He has admittedly failed to do that. He has spent far too much time working on his car in the garage. He has tinkered with his computer and spends too much time doing research on the Internet. He was too tired to engage in conversation when he came home from work. He has coasted in his marriage for years, assuming it would run on fumes rather than on high-octane gasoline—the kind that another man has offered her.

Fourth, *he has failed to deal with his fears of intimacy.* He has not been affectionate with his wife for some time. Again, he thought that he could hide behind, "I'm just not an affectionate kind of guy." This excused him for the moment, but his wife kept score. She tolerated his shortcomings for the past few years as things seemed to worsen, but in the back of her mind she wondered if greater things were in store for her someplace else.

Fifth, *he failed to take responsibility for his sexual difficulties.* For many men who work too hard and ignore personal problems, sexuality suffers. Ben has had erectile difficulties for a number of years but refused to see his doctor because of embarrassment. This is so common for men—we want to avoid doctors of any kind like the plague. We hope problems will disappear without making any real effort to find answers. Then, most often in midlife, the problems rise so high that we can no longer ignore them.

Sixth, *he failed to nurture a diminishing friendship with his wife.* He mistakenly believed that he could offer her a lukewarm friendship when in fact she needed him more now than ever. She wanted a companion to walk with her into the golden years. While he had somehow thought that 35 years together qualified them as friends, he had not put much effort into nurturing their relationship.

A word in physics is appropriate to the situation between Ben and his wife. It is called *entropy*—the idea that things are naturally in a state of decay. Very few things, and certainly not marriage, can be left to survive on their own. A car needs constant tune-ups and oil changes to be kept in good repair. A home needs repainting, yard maintenance, and roof repairs. A marriage is no different. Husbands and wives must constantly work to keep a relationship strong and vibrant. Ben, and to a certain extent, his wife, failed to accomplish that. Now, in midlife, he is paying a large bill.

Kyle's Story

Kyle's story is different from Ben's. He too is in midlife and is facing unique challenges. However, Kyle's situation is one with which most of us can more readily identify.

Kyle has been married for nearly his entire adult life. He is 50 and married Kerry 30 years ago after they'd dated for two years. He came to see me after he tired of trying to sort things out on his own. He had never seen a psychologist before and was wary of the experience. Yet he wanted someone with whom he could share his inner struggles.

Kyle was a contractor with a reputation for building fine homes. He had gone through times of feast and famine, times when he had plenty of work and others when he had to scrape by on small remodel jobs. He worked hard, and it showed in his weathered face and hands. He had a ruddy complexion, typical of someone who has spent years outside in the Pacific Northwest.

Kyle was friendly but quite somber when he told me of his situation.

Kyle and Kerry have survived many problems throughout their marriage. Kerry had an affair with a coworker 20 years ago. She and Kyle had sought the counsel of their pastor and felt they had moved beyond it. They weathered the injury Kyle suffered on a construction site, falling 20 feet and breaking his back. He was off work for more than a year, and their finances suffered severely. The injury continues to plague Kyle, and he must regularly seek help from specialists.

Yet through all their ups and downs, Kyle and Kerry remained active in their church and maintained a close spiritual connection to one another. They have prided themselves in weathering the storms and coming out the other side. They have raised three fine children—two are off to college, and the third has entered the military. They have three grandchildren and have purchased a lot at a resort in the eastern part of the state where they hope to build a vacation and retirement home.

With all this going for them, you might think they are poised for the next stage in their life. Except it is not the stage that you might expect. This stage is one that Kyle is experiencing on his own. It has snuck up on him and threatens to destroy their marriage.

For Kyle, this stage includes worrying about retirement and the financial feasibility of the vacation house they want to build at the resort. Those thoughts swirl constantly in his mind. But there is more. Kyle is overwhelmed with thoughts of whether or not he still loves Kerry, whether or not he wants to embark on another career, whether or not the church they have attended for the past 20 years is still right for him, whether or not he still believes the things the church has taught, whether or not his body will sustain him as he tries to keep up with his buddies at the gym and work site, whether or not he will be able to find the solution to the erectile problems he has experienced the past two years. He wonders about a lot of things that he has not shared with anyone.

How are Kyle's worries impacting him and his marriage?

As you might have guessed, Kyle has developed a low-grade depression so typical of many men. He continues to go to work every day, still attends church, and enjoys his children and grandchildren. But he is not really happy. He is unsure of how to approach the rest of his life. He is at a crossroads, one he keeps hidden from his wife. Kerry senses his discouragement but meets with defensiveness when she tries to broach the subject with him. He sees it differently.

"I have tried to tell her that I'm not happy, but she's so busy with her thing that I am not sure she really hears me. She has been teaching school for nearly 30 years and loves her work. She doesn't seem to have time for me. She complains that I don't seem happy, but I don't think she hears me when I tell her the things that bother me. I tell her that I want more time from her, but she becomes defensive. So now I don't tell her, and that's why I'm here."

Kyle has the blues—the kind that often come from midlife issues. He has the blues that come from being dissatisfied with one's marriage. He has the blues that come from feeling like life is passing him by and time is running out on his dreams and unmet aspirations. He feels the blues that come from holding in all the different feelings that are common to midlife, with no one to share what he experiences. Even worse, he does not know how to change things.

Sadly, most men in Kyle's situation (and there are many) suffer silently. They immerse themselves in distractions that we have already talked about in this book. They buy more Grisham novels. They drink more and enjoy it less. They carry on secret fantasies that are titillating but offer no real joy. They watch their spiritual lives deteriorate. They allow friendships to wither. The blues worsen, and their relationships become stale.

Iron John

A story from the Grimm brothers has been used over the years to illustrate men's necessary journey. It is the story of Iron John, or Iron Hans. It was reportedly first set down around 1820 but may be much older. In his first full-length book, *Iron John*, poet Robert Bly tells the story.

The tale begins with something strange happening in the forest near the king's castle. When hunters go into this area, they disappear and never come back. Those who go to rescue them also fail to return.

One day, an unknown hunter shows up at the castle and asks for a dangerous deed he can do.

> The king says, "Well, I could mention the forest, but there's a problem. The people who go out there don't come back. The return rate is not good."
>
> "That's just the sort of thing I like," the young man says. So he goes into the forest alone, taking only his dog. The young man and his dog wander about in the forest, and they go past a pond. Suddenly, a hand reaches up from the water, grabs the dog, and pulls it down.
>
> The young man doesn't become hysterical. He merely says, "This must be the place."
>
> The hunter goes back to the castle, rounds up three men with buckets, and then comes back to empty the pond. What they find, lying at the bottom of the pond, is a large man covered with hair from head to toe. The hair is reddish—it looks like rusty iron. They take the man back to the castle and imprison him. The King puts him in a cage in the courtyard, calls him "Iron John" and gives the key to the keeping of the Queen.

The point of the story is that a wild man is deep inside all of us and that we must dip into the pond lest we find ourselves at midlife with unfinished business sneaking up and grabbing us. Bly says that the job of all men is to go down into the pond and to accept what they find there.[1]

Bly's message is similar to that of John Eldredge in his book *Wild at Heart.* Something wild and often hidden in a man needs to be "bucketed" out.

And what does this have to do with midlife? Midlife is a fertile time when men are tuned to their emotions, physiology, and spirituality. It is a time when relationships are prone to dissolution because of unfinished business. Men are more awake at midlife than at other times in their lives.

Both Kyle and Ben are alert to what is happening around them and are ready to listen to what might be calling them. It is "stuff" that they must understand if they are to deal successfully with relational issues and other emotional challenges. The blues often come to men who have not been alert and awake for many years. Suddenly, most often in midlife, they find themselves off course and lost.

Women Know

I believe that in many cases, a woman can see into a man's life and intuitively know that he has "stuff" buried in the deep ponds of his psyche. I cannot tell you how many women have come to me for counseling to tell me that their man has so much unfinished business. In spite of the fact that they too may be navigating treacherous midlife waters, women seem able to view their issues while keeping an eye on their man's struggles as well.

As a woman, you know. You know that he has not done his work with his father. You know that he has a father wound that is not healed. You know that he has anger and resentment toward family members that he has not worked through. You watch him avoid doing the dredge work and feel helpless to change his course. You watch his longtime friendships slip away and wonder why he lets them go. As you watch his disposition deteriorate, you want him to rise up, take control of his life, and offer some masculine leadership in your marriage. All too often, it does not happen.

Gordon Dalbey, author of *Healing the Masculine Soul,* believes that women often know what men need to do, but men must learn it for themselves.

> The woman thereby longs for her man to desire and seize his own manly sensitivity, because she knows that the only kind she can release in him is her own—which can meet her where she is, true, but cannot take her where she needs to go…. In a very real sense, therefore, every woman is a princess held captive by a wicked stepmother—the false feminine maternal-source which would keep her bound as a self-centered child. She longs for a prince who is both strong and bold enough to cut her free from that falseness, so that she can be restored to the "true mother" as it were—the root of authentic femininity.[2]

But it is not enough that you know. It is not enough that you can see the work that men need to do. Men need to do the work! They need to step up to the plate before it is too late. Again, Dalbey encourages men: "Standing before the woman in strength of manly sensitivity is no small task for a man today.…

The man who would lift the sword of truth before the woman must be submitted to his God and seeking to please Him alone."[3]

Men and women must bridge an uneasy alliance. Many women know their man is in trouble, yet men must inevitably fight their own battles if they are to earn respect and dignity. Women can serve as helpmates to men, allowing them the freedom to fight and win some of their own battles. It is, to say the least, a difficult situation.

Crises of Midlife for Men

Midlife is a unique time for men and women. It is a time of reflection and struggle. It is a time when we stop to assess where we have been and where we are going. It has been called "midlife crisis." However, we could also call it midlife transition, for it is often a time of adjustments. It is a time to reconsider our choices and change our lifestyles.

It can also be a time of pessimism. When the blues cloud a man's thinking, everything can look bleak. During this time of introspection, male suicide is three times more likely than at any other time in a man's life.

Midlife is a challenging time for all, but why is it so often a time of depression for men? According to Arch Hart, midlife blues have several causes.[4]

A Crisis of Values

Midlife is a time to reevaluate your values. Issues men may have partially addressed in their adolescence return to the surface. Questions about identity come back to haunt them. *Who am I? What do I value?* Midlife is a time when we question the meaning of life. It is a time when we may lose confidence in our abilities and our previously accepted perspectives.

This is a time when women can be incredibly helpful to men. Women can provide ballast for a boat that is listing. They can be an anchor in the storm. Men in midlife will need a sounding board to listen to their anxieties about the future. They may need women to remind them of God's faithfulness in their lives. At a time when things a man once held sacred seem less certain, he needs to know that God provides the answers to life's questions.

A Crisis in Marriage

As we saw in the lives of Ben and Kyle, a marriage crisis may be overt and terrifying, or subtle and worrisome. Either way, it is a crisis, and it must be dealt with.

For many, the crisis in midlife will require relearning how to navigate the path of friendship with a partner. With children grown, the mortgage paid, and other anchors loosened, men may feel as if they are drifting in their marriage.

Women can be immensely helpful here as well. You will often recognize the problem before a man does. You can reach out to your man and precipitate the work of renewing vows and friendship activities. As we discussed in the last chapter, your circle of acquaintances can be useful as you use this time to renew old friendships and build new ones. You can use your intuition and knowledge to spur him to reignite the spark in your marriage. You can offer opportunities to get away to reconnect with one another. You can tell him clearly, honestly, that a rift in your relationship needs attention. You have a chance to create a greater intimacy than ever before.

A Crisis with Children

The children are grown and choosing their own life course. Some make healthy choices, and their parents are proud. For others, the choices are disastrous and discouraging.

Many fathers face this time with concern. Often they have been absent and lack the underpinnings of a strong relationship with their children. The alienation they feel from their children intensifies and brings on the blues. Because they feel the distance and know it is largely their own doing, the guilt they experience during this time can be great indeed.

Women can help men through this challenging time of transition. Because they are "nest builders" and often have a stronger relationship with the children than the father does, they can encourage and foster the rebuilding of father-child relationships. They can encourage men to use small moments to create a lasting friendship with their children.

A Crisis in Career

Many men reach midlife feeling disillusioned about their work. They commonly reach a crisis point—they simply do not want to face another day at the mill or office. What they need is very difficult but not impossible to attain—a sabbatical. They need to take a few weeks and decide what they want to do about their career.

I have come to appreciate a particular approach to finding and doing our best work. It is called "right liveliness." Some universities are teaching it. It essentially means that men must take time to understand what brings meaning to their lives and then make career choices accordingly.

Unfortunately, most men don't take the time to consider what brings meaning to their lives. They have not spent time in prayer and reflection, asking God for understanding. Quite the opposite—most men slip into an occupation by chance. Early in life, they took a job that paid well, and they decided that was good enough. After working for several years, they realize they are stuck. Now, in midlife, they are asking themselves if their job brings them the satisfaction and meaning God intended.

When the meaning in a man's work has evaporated, a real crisis ensues. Obviously, when men have invested a lifetime becoming proficient in their life's work, shifting gears is very difficult. Yet that may be what they need. If so, they will also need a great deal of encouragement and support from their spouse to make the necessary changes.

Other men may need a less drastic step. In many instances, an adjustment in spiritual perspective can bring about a radical life change at the work site. Let me illustrate.

Darren was a 45-year-old sawyer at a local mill. He had been there for 20 years, working his way up from the green chain to lead sawyer. He took pride in meticulously managing the blades that cut the rough timber. Production at the mill was highly dependent on how well he did his job.

In recent years, however, Darren became increasingly irritated and annoyed with his coworkers. He grew to hate the mill politics. He had no patience for men who talked behind his back or bosses who didn't carry their weight. He was frustrated when people called in sick. When he talked to me, he had all but decided to quit his job and find a new profession.

Together we reviewed his work history. He had always enjoyed the prestige of being one of the fastest, smartest sawyers.

It was a unique job that required a high level of expertise, and the men in the mill admired him for his performance. He had always been outgoing and had shared his faith frequently. In recent years, however, he had become withdrawn. He had quit witnessing to others and had dropped out of a noon Bible study.

Together we looked at his life and determined that he was experiencing a biochemical depression that had resulted in his withdrawn behavior. When we addressed this issue with the proper medication, his attitude shifted at work, and he once again began to see that his work was his personal mission field. As he shared his faith more openly and rejoined the Bible study, his work life improved drastically. He reoriented his thinking to see that the mill was a place where he could still feel worthwhile and find meaning—even if things did not always flow smoothly.

Many men will experience a work crisis. Some will need to decide whether they need to change their careers, but most can find contentment by simply tweaking their jobs or other areas of their lives that may be impacting how they feel at work. They may simply need to find ways to create new challenges. The key is to learn to focus not on their external performance but on their inner character and spiritual nature.

A Crisis with Aging Parents

As the life span increases, a growing number of people experience a role reversal with their parents. As Hart explains, "Just about the time when one feels a newfound freedom from not having to take care of children, a new set of responsibilities may emerge. With advancing age, parents begin to decline physically and gradually move back to the helplessness of childhood."[5]

This change can cause adults, especially men, to feel constricted and out of control. Most women seem to navigate toward the role of nurturers, but men generally shun these responsibilities. This transition can be a challenging time for men who must set healthy boundaries while also taking on appropriate responsibilities for parents. The balance can sometimes be hard to find, but here again women can be helpful. They can help men face the challenge of aging parents without necessarily drastically altering their newfound lifestyle. Again, this requires seizing small opportunities, perhaps family gatherings, to keep the relationship strong with parents.

A Crisis of Letting Go

As I look around, I see men in midlife still trying desperately to hang on to vestiges of youth. The headlines are full of stories of men acting like boys. They don't want to slow down in the business world or on the rock-climbing wall. Middle-aged men might boast, "Anything a kid can do, a man can do better." And so, those of us in midlife kill ourselves trying to work as many hours as we did 20 years ago, attempting to run as fast as ever, hiking farther than before, maintaining the sexual prowess of youth. We feel as if letting go would mean failing, but we must do so.

Sexuality—now there is a loaded topic. Often men are unwilling to face the physical changes in their bodies. They are unwilling to face the fact that "*men*-opause" actually exists.

Hart discusses the symptoms of male menopause, technically called andropause. He indicates that men may experience the following symptoms:

- "sore body syndrome" and stiffness

- other physical symptoms, such as hot flashes, headaches, insomnia, and reduced lean body mass
- poor recovery from exercise
- depression, irritability, or lack of motivation
- loss of interest in normal activities
- fatigue
- weight gain
- changes in libido and sexual responsiveness

Even with all that bad news, an opportunity arises. Robert Pasick, in his book *Awakening from the Deep Sleep,* says that midlife is also a time to let go of misconceptions about sexuality. It can be a time to embrace changes and emerge healthier and more alive than ever. He says that we can rid ourselves of...

- prevailing myths about sexuality, such as believing that sex equals intercourse
- a lack of understanding about our sexual desires and needs
- old sexual wounds
- a lack of communication with your spouse about sexuality[6]

Far too many men today struggle with "letting go" of youth. They do not move gracefully into midlife and beyond. They sometimes express legitimate needs and desires in illegitimate ways, such as pornography and affairs. Men steadfastly refuse to face their wounds, let go of them, and experience healing. Addressing this problem can reduce heartache and depression for men.

How can women help? By carrying on a free and open dialogue with men about their needs, by examining ways of finding mutual pleasure together, and by helping to ease men of the burden of sexual obsession.

A Crisis of Faith

Midlife is a time of questioning. It is another season, sometimes called the second adolescence, when men scrutinize what they once accepted. That often includes matters of faith.

We have all known strong Christian leaders who, in midlife, have abandoned their moral principles and acted in ways they would previously have found abhorrent. We have seen pastors leave the ministry because they have deep questions about the tenets of faith they previously clung to. Fortunately, every crisis also provides an opportunity for maturity and self-development. The apostle James tells us to consider it joy when we encounter trials of many kinds, knowing that they can deepen our faith (James 1:2-4). Even moments of darkest depression, when we question whether or not God is there, can be tremendous times of growth.

Soul Work, Depression, and Midlife

During the first half of our lives, we are often involved in creating what the famous psychologist C.J. Jung has called the *persona*. According to Jung, we want acceptance from others so badly that we essentially become what others want us to be. We arduously create this false identity, the persona, to please others.

And we settle for a superficial and shallow existence.

Fortunately, the second half of life offers us a chance to find our authentic selves. The search is not easy; it often involves soul work—creating a mature faith and determining what we believe about God and our relationship to Him. It involves finding meaning where it did not exist before. It involves understanding other people according to scriptural principles.

L. Patrick Carroll and Katherine Marie Dyckman, in their superb book, *Chaos or Creation,* offer us another perspective of depression in midlife. It is based on soul work.

> At midlife, I am called to a greater interiority and to a recognition of my deeper identity based not on "should" and "ought" but on the freedom of the daughters and sons of God....The more I know and pursue my own deepest desires, and take responsibility for actions flowing from them, the sooner the depression will disappear. Usually when I experience depression, I need to be more independent of approval from others and more trusting in God and self.[7]

These authors repeat what we know to be true: "In him we live and move and have our being" (Acts 17:28).

Women can help men with this soul work. You can share your spirituality with your man. You can encourage him to join you in developing your faith together. This may mean taking classes together at church, participating in a new worship experience, or seeking faith-building groups that appeal to both of you. It may be something as simple as experiencing the Sabbath in a different way or praying more regularly at meals.

Midlife Opportunities

For all of its chaos and confusion, midlife is filled with opportunities. It can be a wonderful time for exploration and for finding our authentic selves.

It is interesting to watch the transformation of men as they pass through the treacherous waters of midlife. Some become waylaid, but most make it safely to the other side. Those who would travel safely would do well to follow the guidance of Arch Hart. He says, "Pray for a deep sense of understanding of what is going on within your spirit. Periods of doubt are normal for humans who 'only see through a glass darkly.' Remember, this is your crisis, not God's. This is a time for Him to do His finest work in you, if you cooperate."[8]

As you consider midlife opportunities for your partner, let's reflect on the life of Peter. In Peter's early years he was brash, confident, and trusting in his own resources. In the words of Carroll and Dyckman, he trusted in "a sword he did not need, a courage he did not have."[9] They could have been talking about any number of young men out to prove themselves—all with a disingenuous sense of self. The false bravado that most men have experienced. Puffing ourselves up on the outside to cover what is missing within.

But the circumstances of life changed Peter. Rather than working on problems, maintaining a superficial, external perspective, he sat in the crucible of life, letting problems work on him. He walked with the Lord during those training years, and he evidently learned a great deal. Finally, he experienced the agonizing death, three-day entombment, and exultant resurrection of Christ. He seemed to grow up during this tempestuous time.

Christ later asks Peter if he loves Him "more than these." He can only say, "You know that I love you" (John 21:15). In this context Christ says, "When you were younger you dressed yourself and went where you wanted; but when you are old you will stretch out your hands, and someone else will dress you and lead you where you do not want to go" (21:18).

For all his troubles, Peter grew deeper in ways that he might not have if he had remained full of himself—his false self. Peter witnessed the healing of paralysis and blindness, the feeding of the multitude, the raising of the dead. He watched the Lord overcome the power of hell and Satan and rise triumphantly. In the book of Acts, we see Peter giving what he has in the name of Jesus (Acts 3:6). He has softened. He is confident not in himself but in the Spirit of God. His power comes not from something that he can muster, as in the old days, but from the Lord.

Peter gives us hope.

You can trust that with hard work your man will soften his egocentric perspective and lean more and more on the power of the living Christ. You can maintain hope that the darkest days of self-doubt will give rise to a new assurance as he finds his authentic self. With your help, midlife turmoil will give way to midlife peace.

chapter 8

Walking on Eggshells: Depression and the Family

No man is an island, entire of itself.

—JOHN DONNE

WHAT DOES A MAN BRING HOME WITH HIM in the evening? (No, this is not a dumb joke or a trick question.) What follows him into the family residence after work? What does his family sense before he has uttered a word?

Give up?

His mood!

Many men today bring an unwanted companion home to the family—a mood that is shadowy and dark. It is the monkey on his back that he cannot seem to shake, the monkey the family dreads seeing and hearing. Everyone picks up on it although they rarely talk about it openly. They don't dare.

Consider the dialogue of an old sitcom. See if you sense the mood in the room.

"Edith, where are my slippers? Did you move my slippers? They were sitting right here by the couch last night. You must have moved them," Archie says. He walks around the room muttering to himself.

"They're right where you left them, Archie. Right by the bed," Edith says.

"I don't see them. You must have moved them," he says with increased irritation.

"No, Archie. I'll get them for you."

Many of us recognize this scene, or one like it, from *All in the Family*, the television series that took us into the lives of Archie and Edith Bunker. We smiled at the redneck attitude Archie displayed on a regular basis, and at Edith's tolerant and indulgent style. We laughed at his stiff and difficult personality and the way the family danced around his moods.

As we look back now on the many hilarious episodes of Archie and his family, perhaps we should look through different eyes. Perhaps we should be more critical of how Edith placated Archie and how he demanded his way on most issues. Perhaps we should consider the possibility that Archie was, like many men today, unhappy. Perhaps he too had the blues.

Women watching that show today would undoubtedly react more passionately than they did when the show aired in the 70s. As you reflect on the show, I suspect that you wonder why Edith put up with a schmuck like Archie. I suppose we can write it off to the fact that this was television. The show was designed for ratings and reactions and received both.

But this make-believe scenario can help us understand the effect of the angry, depressed man on his family. Our task for this chapter is to determine if your man might have the blues and, if so, how they might be impacting him, you, and your children.

Sadly, far too many families have an "Archie" as the man in the family. Far too many men, like Archie, are not the happiest people around. Archie certainly exhibited many of the characteristics we have come to associate with the blues: irritability, impatience, low self-esteem, and limited friendships.

Before we look more closely at the impact of depression on the family, let's focus on how the healthy family functions.

Healthy Family Functioning

John Bradshaw has done a great deal of seminal research on the family. His PBS series, *On the Family*, was a huge success in the 90s. He was one of the first to tell us things we did not really want to know about how dysfunctional families behave.

For us to adequately understand the impact of male depression on the family, we must first understand how a healthy family works. A healthy and fully functioning family is a place where things work.

Bradshaw says this in his popular book *Bradshaw On: The Family*:

> A functional, healthy family is one in which all the members are fully functional and all the relationships between the members are fully functional. As human beings, all family members have available to them the use of all their human powers. They use these powers to cooperate, individuate and get their collective and individual needs met. A functional family is the healthy soil out of which individuals can become mature human beings.

This involves several characteristics:

- The family ensures each member's survival and growth.

- The family meets the emotional needs of family members. These include a balance between autonomy and dependency as well as social and sexual training.

- A healthy family nurtures each member of the family, including the parents, helping them develop.

- A healthy family creates the atmosphere for developing self-esteem.

- The family is a place where we are socialized, learning etiquette and other skills for living in a civilized world.[1]

Let's now take a closer look at the Bunker family and consider how functional it was.

The Typical Family

We may have left the Bunkers back in the 70s, but unfortunately we have maintained much unhealthy family functioning. A lot of "Archies" are still around, as are plenty of young and middle-aged men who are far less than happy and who scream out their frustration with life.

We also see too many homes where the father calls people names. The oldest child often takes the brunt of his father's bad moods head-on. When we consider the importance of a name and the impact labels have on children, we cringe when hearing a mother or father calling a child a derogatory name out of frustration.

An evening walk through Wal-Mart reveals much about typical family life. On a recent outing I stopped for a moment near the entry to the giant store and listened to parents talk to their children. You know what I heard because you have heard it as well. Parents treated children as cattle; they prodded them to hurry up, slow down, hold hands, let go. Parents bark out orders like a drill sergeant, and children either fearfully obey or wildly act out their confusion and fear.

Name-calling has a tremendously negative impact on a child. When Archie called his son-in-law, Mike, Meathead, he labeled him as stupid, and that is a tragedy for anyone. The psychological scarring is unseen but very real. It tears at the fabric of the personality and the self-esteem that we want for our children. One wonders how Mike would feel about himself in real life with that kind of name tagged to him. Certainly the family was not a place where he could grow, feel safe to share his emotional needs, and develop the self-esteem that could carry him through life.

You might wonder at the motivation of parents who fall into name-calling. Certainly the reasons are varied, ranging from their early learning and low self-esteem to their lack of self-confidence and limited relational skills. Certainly the effective parent has learned other parenting skills that do not demean the children and that help the parents feel better about their role as parents.

We know that names can hurt. Sarcasm causes pain, and humiliation damages the emerging personality. Research has shown that verbal abuse is even more debilitating to a child and their self-esteem than intermittent physical abuse. We can surmise that Archie would have learned this kind of treatment from his father.

Gary Smalley and John Trent, in their powerful book *The Blessing,* share how critical the parents' blessing is for their children. These authors indicate that children are desperate for affirmation and will be damaged without it. Children need to hear that they are unique, valued, and special to the family. Parents must recognize and affirm children's unique attributes. Many fathers fail this test with their children.

As we watch many families in action, we wonder why women do not stand up to their husbands. Why do they allow them to call their children such horrible names? Why don't they intervene somehow?

I can attest to this dilemma.

Recently, I worked with a woman who acted frightened of her husband. She literally cowered in his presence. She measured and considered every word she said. I quickly learned about verbal abuse in the family and realized that she had learned to walk carefully around her husband. Many women choose to live that way for fear of being lambasted. Once bitten, twice shy.

Escape into Codependency

Edith clearly did her own dance to stay out of Archie's range. At times, she seemed to be in another world—perhaps that was her way of coping with a man who seemed to have the blues and who was more than willing to share them. She escaped into codependency, using all of her skills and energies to please her man. It was a way to cope. The world revolved around Archie, and he left no extra room for anyone else's problems, feelings, or concerns. This is often the case in families where a man has the blues and refuses help for them.

Edith demonstrated the role of a codependent. People in survival mode learn to be on guard. They learn to live from the outside in. They must constantly be vigilant to what is happening outside their own life. Bradshaw states, "Codependence is always a symptom of abandonment...including neglect, abuse and enmeshment. Codependence is a loss of one's inner reality and an addiction to outer reality."[2]

In Terrence Reals' book *I Don't Want to Talk About It*, he describes what we might be seeing in Edith's character. He says,

> If the relationship of most traditional wives to their breadwinning men is one of caretaking, of "building up the male ego," then the wife's relationship to a depressed spouse represents a kind of caretaking doubled. Wives of depressed men tend to blame themselves; they try to cajole their husbands into getting help. They may nag; they may complain. But until things get truly dismal, they seldom put their foot down.[3]

In *All in the Family*, Mike was married to Archie and Edith's daughter, Gloria, the effervescent blonde. A little dingy (just like Edith), Gloria was outgoing and bubbly. She grew up to be much like her mother, enabling her father to be his gruff, grouchy self. We rarely see her stand up for her husband unless he has taken a stand first himself.

Is Gloria happy? How has her grousing, argumentative, depressed father affected her? We are left to wonder. On the face of things, she appears relatively unscathed. But we know better. We know that an angry, depressed man can chill the warmest of homes. He can send any errant emotions running. Perhaps that is what we see in Gloria—the bright, funny one who functioned as the distracter. She kept the family from asking the huge question that was on everyone's mind: What's wrong with Daddy?

For all of her liveliness, Gloria does not escape her father's sarcastic bite. She too is put in her place. It is Dad's way or no way. He runs the show and expects Gloria, Mike, and Edith to adjust to his moods. They can be happy if he is happy. But if he is not happy, beware.

And so we see the Bunkers in a new light. Again, we wonder, was Archie depressed? Did he have the blues? He was certainly the kind of man that would never talk about his emotions openly. He was the epitome of the man who made it clear that his moods were off-limits to any conversation or examination. He suffered silently while the family scrambled to find the survival skills necessary to deal with his moods—all the while walking on eggshells.

Certainly not all women today are passive, mousy doormats, ready to wait anxiously on their man hand and foot. In fact, such an image may make you cringe. But not so fast. The passive style is not the only version of codependency. Another variety is also common. Some family members are so nervous about getting walked on that they erect steel bars on the edges of their lives so that no one will hurt them. They might as well wear sandwich boards that blast the warning, "Don't mess with me!" Women who fit this description are rough, tough, and ready for action. But tragically, they will not only avoid the bad that comes from a man's moods and actions but also miss out on the good. They will allow no one close enough to hurt them or to nurture them. Might you have erected some of these rigid boundaries to prevent you from feeling his darts of disapproval? Has intimacy been painful, causing you to withdraw into your own lonely world?

Men are not created all alike. They come in different shapes and personalities. I am reminded of two very different coaches for my son's Little League team. One, Josh Thompson, was a cranky, irritable, scruffy-haired man who seemed intent on making the kids tremble with fear when he called their names. He never used a child's first name. It was always, "Hey, Johnson, get over here." Or "White, go over and play second base." If a child ever tossed the ball to the wrong base, failed to catch a pop fly, or (heaven forbid) struck out at the plate, Josh seemed to take it personally. Little wonder that several of the kids dropped out of baseball before the end of the season. They didn't want to be around an unhappy man when they were trying to have fun.

Then there was Tim Dennehy. Tim would be at the ballpark before any of the kids, and the first thing he did when they arrived was pass around a bag of Big League Chew bubble gum for the kids to share. Sometimes he brought sunflower seeds; always he brought a big, contagious smile with plenty of compliments. "Donny, you looked hot up at the plate. Bobby, where did you learn to hit like that?" The only thing he asked from the kids was a smile in return. They couldn't get enough time with Mr. Dennehy.

Kids know what is going on with adults. They are like little sensors that pick up vibrations on the ball field or in the home. They know when parents are happy, and they know when the tension is so thick it can be cut with a knife. They are affected by everything that happens around them.

Bradshaw on the Family

John Bradshaw would, I am sure, be very critical of the Bunker family and any family where warmth and intimacy cannot exist. He would say that the Bunkers, and families like them, fail to meet the needs of its individual members, including the men. Because of men's troubles, they are unable to grow or to develop emotional maturity. Undoubtedly, their problems started in the families they grew up in.

One of the goals of the healthy family is to produce healthy, mature individuals. Bradshaw has some insights to share on this topic as well.

> A mature person is one who has differentiated himself from all others and established clearly marked ego boundaries. A mature person has a good identity. Such a person is able to relate to his family system in meaningful ways without being fused or joined to them. This means that one is emotionally free and can choose to move near without anger or absorption and move away without guilt.[4]

Each person in the family needs to find his or her unique place in the family and world. I love the verse that says, "Train a child in the way he should go, and when he is old he will not turn from it" (Proverbs 22:6). Many believe that this verse instructs us to listen to our children for their "natural bents"— those interests and talents that make each of them a unique creation. Allow them the freedom to be who God designed them to be. Is your home a place where each child is free to express his or her talents and gifts?

The home must be a place of safety where individuals can risk growth and individual expression. With the proper affection and recognition, individuals can branch out on their own while hanging on to the trunk of the family for security.

I hope your family mood is not one of fear or apprehension, as so often results from untreated depression. I hope the mood is not one of anger, shame, or overriding guilt. I hope your home is filled with joy. As Bradshaw states, "Joy is the energy that signals all is well. All needs are being filled. One is becoming and growing. Joy creates boundless energy." [5]

Vain Conceit and Selfish Ambition

Depression, left untreated, can be all consuming. Untreated depression is, in many respects, a form of vain conceit and selfish ambition. Let me explain.

Consider with me the people who insist that every wrong they have done, no matter how slight, is an egregious matter. They try to convince you that their actions are the worst sins anyone could ever commit. How do you feel when you sit with someone who tells you that absolutely nothing is redeemable about their character? If you are like me, you feel slightly annoyed. You have to tell yourself not to reach out and shake these inconsolable ones and tell them that they are seriously misinformed. No, they are not the worst of the worst. Not only are they redeemable, but other people like and appreciate them.

The reasons for your annoyance are many. You see the falsehood behind what they are saying. You know that they are deceived. Perhaps you also sense the subtle narcissism in such a grand statement as, "No one is more unlovable than I am." You want to say, "Stop feeling sorry for yourself!"

In the same way, people with untreated depression may be filled with conceit. They may have decided that their malady, the blues, is more important than the overall functioning of the family. Perhaps they have selfishly decided to ignore the needs of the family so they can mope around, stuck in their muddle.

Lest I sound insensitive to men with depression, I am limiting my focus to those who fail to acknowledge and wrestle with their blues. I am critical of those who selfishly decide that they are above seeking help from a qualified psychologist or medical doctor. I am annoyed at the men who set their families up for needless suffering.

In Philippians 2:3-4, the apostle Paul said, "Do nothing out of selfish ambition or vain conceit, but in humility consider others better than yourselves. Each of you should look not only to your own interests, but also to the interests of others." Notice that he did not say to ignore your needs. He encourages you to take care of yourself but also to show due concern for others.

Consider how this verse applies to the family of the depressed man. Consider what it says to the person consumed by anger and self-pity. Many men struggle needlessly in silence, and in the process, drag their families along with them.

The passage written by the apostle Paul goes on to hold up Jesus' example:

"Your attitude should be the same as that of Christ Jesus: who, being in very nature God, did not consider equality with God something to be grasped, but made himself nothing, taking the very nature of a servant, being made in human likeness. And being found in appearance as a man, he humbled himself and became obedient to death—even death on a cross!" (Philippians 2:5-8).

We see that Christ epitomized selflessness. Paul explains that Christ gave up His powers of deity to become a man—bearing the scorn and shame of humanity and dying a horrific death on the cross. Christ gave up any pride so that He could save a lost world.

The question for us is much more limited in scope: Can men give up false humility to help their families?

Learning to Dance

Kate was a petite professional woman who came to see me after experiencing years of what she called "verbal abuse" from her husband. She told me that things had gotten worse in the past few years, and she felt depressed. She had lost more than 20 pounds and appeared gaunt and tired, as evidenced by her sunken cheeks and the dark circles under her eyes.

Kate described her ten-year marriage to Bob, a prominent attorney, as "very difficult after the first three years." According to Kate, her husband had become depressed early in their marriage and refused any help for it. He became increasingly angry, sullen, and critical of her. She shared the following story.

One night, after arguing briefly, Bob slammed the bedroom door on his way out. She had asked if he had felt pushed away when she said she was exhausted, too tired for intimacy. She explained that she had to get up at 5:30 to get to work.

According to his version, he just "closed it firmly." Kate followed him out to the living room to try to patch things up. It was late, and she was so tired. Her thoughts were filled with the demands of the next day, yet she felt the need to take care of this crisis. She hated having him upset with her. It could mean days of pouting and silence.

She began their predictable dance. Kate asked what was wrong. Bob said, "Nothing!" When she asked why he had left the room and slammed the door, he remained distant and cool. "Nothing's wrong, Kate. Just go back to bed."

"I'm not mad," he again proclaimed. She tried to spark a conversation, but in her exhausted state, she felt as if she were trying to climb a mountain in tennis shoes. The conversation bogged down. She was frightened, and her breathing was shallow. What would happen next? It could be anything from stilted silence to an utter explosion.

Kate had been trying to fix things for all ten years of their marriage. Bob exhibited all the symptoms of a depressed man. She exhibited all the symptoms of a card-carrying caretaker:

- She always watched out for his feelings to see if she had done anything wrong.
- She changed her plans and needs to "fix" the immediate problem.
- She had lost touch with her feelings and given up her goals for her life.
- She wanted to please him and keep the peace.
- She enabled him to continue his inappropriate behavior.
- She was liked by everyone but him.

Kate was a classic codependent. She was always watching his feelings and scanning her actions to see if she had done anything wrong. She cautioned their two children to be careful of their father's moods. Her body was an emotional barometer, tuned to pick up even the slightest change in domestic temperature. She had trouble reading her own feelings but was an expert at knowing what others in the home were feeling. No wonder. Her emotional life depended upon it.

Lately she had been feeling the pressure in the bedroom. Bob said he couldn't help it. He found Kate attractive and was doing what any man would do. He touched her whenever he walked by—a pinch here, a grab there. Kate fantasized about buying protective armor so that his probes would find cold metal instead of her warm body. Each time she had such thoughts, however, she felt guilty. What was wrong with what he was doing? It was what all men did—or so she was told. He wanted her in the bedroom but was withdrawn and angry everywhere else. He rarely asked how she was doing emotionally. He was critical of her and their children, and things seemed tense between Kate and Bob most of the time. These were not the best conditions for intimacy.

Kate could not really understand her feelings. Once very attracted to Bob, she still desired his love and affection. But she now shunned his advances. She had headaches more frequently. She went to bed early to avoid being intimate with him. When they did "make love," she felt as if she was being used. She did not feel loved as a person. She knew that their children feared his angry outbursts. Yet every time she tried to explain this to him, he turned the problem back onto her. She was somehow wrong, and she would pay for it over the course of the next few days.

Kate shared how she felt terribly confused when talking with her husband. She tried to reason with him about his apparent depression, but he denied feeling depressed or angry. Nothing seemed to work. The problem was always hers. He could not see how he had turned their sexual relationship into a matter of duty, which took all of the emotion and soul out of it for her. He would not listen to her complaints that she felt used. This was a huge slap in the face to him, he said. All he wanted was what every other man wanted. Nothing more.

There it was again. "All I want is what every other man wants." Maybe he was right, she thought. She felt confused, alone, and guilty. Where would she turn next?

Breaking the Eggshells

For Kate, the eggshells were beginning to break. She had tolerated his abuse, lived in silence, and rationalized away their pain for a long time. But the rationalizations were no longer assuaging the grief. The membrane on the shell was wearing thin.

Every woman knows when things start their slow decline. She may be confused and uncertain of her choices, but she knows that things are not right. This, truly, is the beginning of change. It starts with a seed and grows stronger with every effort to change.

She knows that she is beginning to break the eggshells when she starts some new behaviors:

- She challenges his beliefs, though unsure of herself.

- She asks her friends if what she is thinking is crazy.

- She journals and listens to God in prayer.

- She says no.

- She seeks counseling.

- She listens to her heart.

For most women, change begins in the heart. This is when you will begin to know that you are not living the way that you can or should be. This is where you will sense your unhappiness and know that change must happen. This stirring can lead you to the truth if you have the courage to listen.

You have read much of this book now and understand depression. You have a good sense about whether your man has the blues. You have a good sense about how it has impacted you and your children. You know that you cannot live like this any longer—you must take action, ever so slowly.

Most women have two very strong fears. One is that they will never be able to change their situation. They fear that no matter how hard they try, they will never have the strength to reach their destination. They fear being stuck in their disappointing life forever.

Their second fear is that they will change and have to face transitions that they are not prepared for. If they never change, they will be lost forever in their place of torment, never able to leave. If they do change, they must gain the strength to walk out of the dark place and fend for themselves. Even with all the support they can garner, they must journey part of the way alone. They will need courage.

You may be frightened of change. Any family is a system; when one part changes, it affects every other part. You know that if your man begins to change, perhaps in response to you changing, the whole family will change.

What will you become? What is to become of the family? When you are clear with him that he must seek help for the blues, how will he respond? These can be frightening questions to consider.

The Embryo

As a young adult, I raised chickens and set out to hatch some of the eggs. Daily I nurtured the embryos, supplying just the right amount of heat and moisture to sustain and enhance life. I marveled at the new life within each egg, which I could see as the days went by.

As I neared the time when the chicks would hatch, it was difficult for me to watch them struggle to emerge from their shells. The weak chicks would peck for such a short time before becoming exhausted, falling back into a restful state until they were ready to try again to peck their way out. I decided that

I could lend a helping hand, making their journey easier and shorter. When the chicks started again to peck their way out, I chipped away at their shells to ease their struggle. I felt a sense of pride that I was helping these weak chicks to enter the world.

The next several hours were shocking and painful to me. Each chick that I had helped out of its shell proceeded to deteriorate and finally die. I was grief stricken. What had I done wrong?

I decided that I would not help the remaining chicks to see if that made a difference. As I patiently watched them struggle against their shells, they finally emerged strong and healthy. I later learned that the chicks needed that part of the journey to become strong enough to live outside their protective shells. The struggle was actually part of the journey, a necessary part that helped to build the strength they needed for life.

You too may feel exhausted with the struggle. You may not be aware that with every movement you are gaining strength to carry you further on your journey. Stay the course! None of the steps are wasted. You have already decided that you deserve a better life, one filled with dignity and safety, and that is the most important decision you can make. You have decided to make changes, and those changes will come. He too deserves a better life, and you can help him first by helping yourself. Let's look at a few action steps you can take.

Recovery and the Family

If you and your children have been living with a man who has the blues, not only does he have some healing to do, but you undoubtedly do as well. As you have read this chapter, perhaps you have recognized some ways you have been affected by his struggles with depression. You know what he needs to do to heal, but what about you? What about your children? First, *remember that you cannot force him to receive help.* You can set some healthy boundaries for yourself and your children, but you cannot control him. Remember to use the communication tools we covered earlier in this book. Be clear, concise, and consistent in the messages you give him.

Second, *talk about it.* Come out of hiding about the family problem. Be willing to seek help, even if he is unwilling. As they say in the 12-step tradition of Alcoholics Anonymous, "You're only as sick as your secrets!" Consider joining a group for families of depressed individuals. As you join others with similar problems, you emerge from isolation and gain support.

Third, *support him in steps he is willing to take to get healthy.* Be informed about depression and lovingly share information with him when he is willing and ready to hear it. Encourage him to talk to someone about his blues. Encourage him to read up on this very treatable problem. (I have cited many helpful books thus far but would like to add the classic *Feeling Good*, by David Burns, as a very readable source on treating depression.) Life can be better for all of you.

Fourth, *practice sharing feelings again.* You can do this with your spouse, with your family, and with your support group. Share your anger and frustration about how his depression has affected the family. Practice journaling as a way of understanding what you are feeling. We should not be welded to our feelings, but they can powerfully help us change.

Fifth, *practice externalizing your shame.* It is not your fault that he has the blues, and it is not your job to fix him. Practice making shame a feeling, not a state of being. As you feel the shame, you can put things in perspective. Give responsibility back to the owner of the problem.

Sixth, *practice tuning in to the emotional needs of your children.* Watch carefully as they begin to take on unhealthy roles. Take care that they do not feel they have to be perfect to avoid criticism, or serve as a distraction to lighten the mood of the home. Encourage them to follow their natural inclinations and gifts.

Last but not least, *pray. Seek God and His counsel.* Listen carefully for any vain ambitions of your own. Listen for indications that you may need to rely less on your own strengths and more on God's.

The Clarion Cry
of the Church

"Who do you love?"

"Jesus!"

"Who do you love?"

"Jesus!"

"Who do you love?"

"Jesus!"

With each chant the voices grew louder and more raucous. At first I wanted to cry out, "The Mariners"—we were in the Kingdome, and we had just ended a winning season—but I soon came to appreciate the enthusiasm of being together with other men to celebrate our common faith.

Still, it was a bit awkward. Men gathering for something other than a baseball game or golf match? Men embracing each other, sharing tears of joy and happiness? What was this I was experiencing? It was just a bit surreal.

It was 1995. Thousands of men, sweaty and gleeful, had packed a baseball and football stadium for something other than sports. Could it be real? What was going on here?

I had traveled to Seattle in a van with a half-dozen others, hoping to find something that was missing from my soul. I wanted to be with other men, share my heart with other men, sing and dance with other men. I love women, but this was a time for the fellowship of men.

So we came—in cars, vans, and buses—and filed into the Dome, past vendors hawking T-shirts, Jesus pins, and posters. We came ready to experience something new. Our van load of enthusiastic believers was similar to hundreds of others filled with men from churches and cities throughout the Northwest. All of us were hoping to fill an empty spot in our souls—and Promise Keepers promised to do the job.

A massive advertising campaign had attracted participants. Bill McCartney, perhaps one of the best football coaches alive, was the point man for the Promise Keepers campaign. Jack Hayford, a mega-church pastor from California, led worship. These men were giants in the larger church, and this was evidence that they knew something powerful was happening and wanted to be part of it.

Promise Keepers seemed to be the church's response to the national men's movement headed by the likes of Robert Bly and Michael Meade. They had burst onto the scene shortly after John Bradshaw exploded into our awareness with his highly celebrated work on the family and addictions. He had written books on family functioning and shame that we were devouring in an attempt to heal our maladies. Our nation was developing a new level of consciousness about our spiritual and emotional deprivation. We were awakening to the possibility that we could not continue down our dark path of self-indulgence.

Robert Bly was a hero—someone men could look to for an answer to their malaise. He dared to be one of the first, and most eloquent, to give a voice to some of the painful issues men face. McCartney was almost a Christian version of Bly. He was someone with biblical underpinnings whom we could turn to for answers to deeper questions about life.

The stadium erupted as Pastor Hayford led us in praise choruses. We were deeply moved as he led us in "Majesty," the song he had written years earlier, and one I had led congregations in singing hundreds of times.

A series of dynamic speakers followed, encouraging us to become men of character. They challenged us to put racial and cultural differences aside and meet in the aisle of unity. They scolded us for our shallowness and pleaded with us to become deeper men of God. We responded with hugs and tears.

As the day wore on, we became increasingly vulnerable. We heard passionate sermons with penetrating questions:

- Were we committed to being better fathers?
- Were we committed to being better husbands?
- Were we committed to laying down racial barriers?
- Were we committed to laying down religious barriers?
- Were we committed to developing a richer relationship with God?

These were good questions. This was one of the first times I had seen my desires to be with men and to worship God come together. We answered the call to become better fathers, husbands, brothers, and neighbors. We promised. It was a start.

Wanting More

I was thankful for this new beginning. Events like this one have been springboards that many churches needed to begin men's ministries. Countless churches I know have formed men's programs following formats offered by Promise Keepers. Many groups have risen out of the initial Promise Keepers push. This has all been good.

Still, men must find ways to keep the momentum going. I am committed to that end. In spite of that commitment, and perhaps surprisingly, I have not gone back to a Promise Keepers' event. I am not sure why. For me, something is missing.

I remember listening to a major Christian radio broadcast talking about the need for men to come clean with their sins of gossip, lack of neighborliness, pride, and jealousy. The speaker challenged us to get together in small Bible studies and share one another's burdens. It all sounded so good, so safe…so sanitized. I knew the sins and addictions in my life, and they were far more severe than gossiping. I wondered if I was some oddball listening to the Christian broadcast. The program seemed superficial and failed to address the place where I lived. I wondered if was the only one who felt this way.

During this time, I looked for my own experience of men coming together. I formed a men's group at my church. Thankfully, my pastor, Jim, saw the same need—to meet with other men in a safe environment and get down to the nitty-gritty issues of life: addictions to work, sex, alcohol, drugs, and gambling; problems with unfaithfulness, isolation, and depression. Why were these same issues not addressed on the major Christian broadcasts? Why didn't those broadcasts address issues like mine?

Why had I never heard a single sermon on male depression, even though it is widespread?

Also during this time, a mainline denominational church in my city pioneered a new and different kind of outreach. (Many churches have started exciting new churches in their own cities.) This new ministry chose not to meet in a church but in a warehouse. The pastor wore jeans and drank soda during his sermon. The congregation sponsored a recovery program for addicts of all kinds. Instead of renting or paying a mortgage, they used their offerings to minister to the needy. They freely offered their money, homes, love, and support. They were willing to talk about depression, anger, unfaithfulness, and other issues in a very "unchurchy" way.

Many distinctive churches are popping up all over America. They meet in odd places, their dress code is unusual, their worship style stretches me, they meet on Saturday nights. They are a breath of fresh air to the larger church family. To date, the parent church in my town has given birth to at least three other churches. The people who serve in these new churches do not seek glory or fame. They are simple folks who talk straight about reality and the message of Jesus. They talk frankly about marriage, love, divorce, loss, depression, and hope without blinking. Their humble church is a refreshing place to consider how Jesus is relevant in the lives of these unique individuals.

In addition to reaching a new group of people, these gatherings are also bringing new life to the parent churches. The non-stereotypical leaders dare to talk about issues that men need to hear. They help men to talk about depression and the addictions and compulsive behaviors that lead up to it. They know that addictions and depression are not sins, that they wreak havoc on marriages, that they sometimes require professional attention.

What can we learn from these off-brand churches and other churches that have dared to break old molds? Have they found a way to construct new bridges between the church and the daily needs of the body and spirit? I believe they have.

Let's look at how the church can take an active role in addressing the needs of men.

The Practical Needs of Men

Men need Christian leaders who offer a clear voice of leadership. At a time when men are wandering, confused about their role in the home as well as in the workplace, men need leadership now more than ever.

Should the church offer leadership in the areas of men's needs? Should the church expand its mission beyond traditional teachings? I think it should. The church is in an influential position to impact men's lives in a positive way. Here are some ideas.

Affiliation

Men are generally social animals and like to affiliate with one another. You see it happening in various service organizations—interestingly, often named after animals—like the Elks, the Moose, and the Lions. These organizations have become fraternities for men, with officers, ranks, and rules of order. Men seem to enjoy that kind of stuff, though I suspect it's just a path to the camaraderie they are really after.

Men like to use the sports world as a focus for congregation. Whether they gather to watch a big baseball or football game, or to play a round of golf, men like to be with one another in an upbeat, competitive atmosphere that includes skill and physical activity.

I have seen churches capitalize on men's love of fellowship to get men thinking about bigger issues. They sponsor men's golf events, Bible studies, and retreats. Most churches offer a variety of opportunities for men to gather with one another.

Achievement

Yes, men are terribly competitive. Ask any man and he will probably admit he wants to know he can match other men's material wealth, talent, education, and strength and fitness. Even his wife can become a point of comparison. Is she as fit as his buddies' wives? Is she as beautiful, talented, and sensuous? Like it or not, these questions are likely to run through a man's mind.

Church leaders can help men understand that this basic drive in men is a gift from God. I have talked to countless men who feel as though their desire to achieve is inappropriate, and they must relegate it to the edges of their lives. They either pretend this drive doesn't exist or they feel ashamed about it. Either way, these men isolate themselves from part of their God-given identity.

Adventure

John Eldredge, author of *Wild at Heart*, has done men a great service by clarifying this need. He paints a picture for us of a God who designed a wild world and peopled it with wild men. "The whole creation is unapologetically wild. God loves it that way....God is a person who takes immense risk. No doubt the biggest risk of all was when he gave angels and men free will, including the freedom to reject him—not just once, but every single day."[1]

Eldredge says, and I agree, that men were made for risk and danger. We were not designed to simply "exist" in safe, sanitized lives. Perhaps that is why we read about men doing wild and crazy things, getting hurt or even killed while performing exploits that, on the surface, don't make sense. But on a deeper level we see that God is wild and crazy too, and He designed us in His image. The Old Testament is replete with examples of God acting boldly, parting the waters, turning rods into serpents, speaking out of a burning bush. You will find nothing tepid about this God.

I have been encouraged to see churches offering backpacking trips into the Washington Cascades or kayaking adventures on Oregon rivers. Many churches offer short-term mission opportunities on foreign soil—this seems particularly appealing to men. Just today I heard a man excitedly talk about his desire to work with orphaned children in Mexico. I see these outings as opportunities for adventure and fellowship.

I confess to having a need for adventure. Even at my age, I like to scream down a dirt path on my mountain bike or feel my small sailboat heel over in the wind, splashing salt water into my eyes. I enjoy taking airplane rides with my friend, Dan, who always adds a dollop of bravado to the flight over Puget Sound and the Olympics.

I decided several years ago that I would take my sons, individually, on Alaskan treks with my father. Each trip was slightly different, but both included elements of excitement, adventure, and danger. We took a floatplane into an isolated lake to do some fishing. As the bush pilot swooped over the Kenai River, we could see grizzly bears feeding not far from where we would be fishing.

"Keep an eye out," he said, "and you'll be all right."

I must say that the thought of a bear bursting from a thicket to snatch the rainbow trout from my line had me worried. But looking back on it, each adventure offered my sons and me bonding time with their grandfather that was far richer than any trip to a drive-in movie or a local bowling alley. This was real-life action—with a little Daniel Boone thrown in.

Admiration

Eldredge says we need a beauty to fight for and then to receive admiration from.

> All of [God's] wildness and all his fierceness are inseparable from his romantic heart. That theologians have missed this says more about theologians than it does about God. Music, wine, poetry, sunsets…those were his inventions, not ours. We simply discovered what he had already thought of. Lovers and honeymooners choose places like Hawaii, the Bahamas, or Tuscany as a backdrop for their love. But, whose idea was Hawaii, the Bahamas, and Tuscany?[2]

We can take a moment to reflect on God, the exquisite lover who woos us into His bosom. He offers the Song of Solomon not only as a metaphor of His love for us but also as a celebration of an aspect of His creation that we are invited to thoroughly enjoy. "Eat, O friends, and drink; drink your fill, O lovers" (Song of Solomon 5:1).

Few things excite a man as much as having his wife welcome him at the door when he comes home at night. If she greets him warmly, gives him a kiss, and tells him how proud she is of him, he will usually melt. He needs to see the twinkle in her eye that says he can still thrill and excite her. He needs to know that he still "has what it takes." Don't kid yourself—if that disappears, something dies in men.

Play

I'm sure you know men who turn everything into work. The depressed man is particularly guilty of this behavior. A golf game becomes an obsession to prove that he can do better and better and better until all the fun is gone.

I recently joined a gym in an attempt to trim some of the bulge from my belly. I am amazed to see how many men spend hours at fitness centers sculpting their bodies. They aren't interested in simply being fit and healthy. Each machine has a purpose for the man who would be Adonis. Each exercise holds a purpose far beyond an aerobic workout. These men are on a mission. They are focused, perhaps even obsessed.

And where is the play? What happened to throwing a Frisbee just because it's a good time? What happened to playing hide-and-seek with our kids or sitting around the piano singing songs with family and friends? Modern life has taken on a severity. Everything is important. Outcome seems to be all that matters.

Again, the church seems a natural place for the antics of men to spring loose. Here, in the safety of other like-minded men, we can let our hair down. We are free to challenge one another at church basketball contests. We can cut up like high school boys when attending the annual men's retreat, a staple at most churches. How delightful it is when the pastor will model frivolity and play by participating in a softball game or volleyball match.

Breaking through the iciness of most men's psyches takes effort. Or perhaps it takes play. It requires taking things far less seriously. Why must we be reminded to have fun?

Meaningful Work

And here you strike at the heart of many men. This is their Achilles heel, so be careful when you wander close. Freud was right when he said two important issues for men were *lieben und arbeiten*—love and work. We have talked about your man's need for love, his need to win the heart of his beauty. Now let's revisit the importance of work.

For many men, work is the yardstick for measuring how they compare with other men. (Like it or not, competition is huge for most of us.) Men look around and compare their career standing and economic status with that of other men. Even more importantly, they want to know that their partner is proud of their accomplishments.

I know a man who works as much overtime as possible at a local mill. Why does he work these extra shifts that make him tired, grouchy, and depressed? The answer is that this is his way of proving that he has worth. Men who see the world as offering too few avenues for earning self-worth often pride themselves on being able to work more doubles than kids half their age. The ability to do so becomes a badge of honor. Even the young bucks are impressed. And the money is good. For someone without a high school diploma, the money is very good.

But does this meet his deep need for "right livelihood" that we talked about previously? Probably not. Many men have made compromises in this area of their lives. Most are doing what they have been taught to do and are sticking with it. Most feel stuck in their profession long after the joy wears off. But, particularly in today's uncertain economic world, they are afraid to change professions.

How has the church helped men with this incredible challenge? I have heard many sermons encouraging men to develop a healthy balance between work and family life. I know of many pastors who strive to be good husbands in spite of tremendous pressure to always be available to their congregants. I admire their resolve.

Perhaps church leaders could also help men find the perfect work for their temperament or make career changes when that need arises. Men will sometimes need to be coached or counseled to discover something that could excite them again professionally. The church is in a position to speak to men in this area.

Passion and Sexuality

Willard Harley, author of *His Needs/Her Needs,* was one of the first to proclaim how important passion, sexuality, and sensuality are to men. Harley claims that passion is one of men's five most important needs. I concur.

I hope I do not need to remind you of this. You know how quickly a man's ego gets bruised if the bedroom is not a warm and inviting place. I also do not need to tell you that he can get irritated about sexuality as quickly as he can about any other important issue. Why? The short answer is that God has created him to be a sexual being. This is a highly personal area, and he can feel rebuffed when things aren't going well.

I know what you are thinking. If it is so important, why doesn't he comprehend a woman's need for emotional nurturance in order to create a proper climate for optimal sexuality? The short answer? I don't know! The title of my previous book, *Men Just Don't Get It,* acknowledges the disconnect between men and their emotional lives. This problem seems to impact their ability, and perhaps even willingness, to reach out emotionally to their partners.

The church has challenged men about the importance of growing up emotionally. Men have often heard about the importance of being available to their mates emotionally and how that will affect the sexual climate in the home. Hearing this from the pulpit offers validity to the issue.

A Place to Grieve

Finally, men need grieving, deep healing, and a safe place to deal with these issues. In previous chapters, I talked about the wounds that men have endured. It is such a vital point that it is worth repeating. This is a tremendous hurdle facing men. However, their wounds are not the problem. It is their pride—their fear of facing the wounds. Please keep in mind our culture has trained men not to show or share our wounds. We have learned to avoid any appearance of weakness or vulnerability. This conditioning is so powerful that it stops us from even acknowledging that we have been hurt.

I firmly believe that before men can come out from behind their protective wall of pride, become vulnerable, and explore their wounds, they must first have a perfectly safe place in which to do so. The church is beginning to be such a place. Men should not have to feel shame for the secrets and pain they harbor. The church must not coddle them but provide them a sanctuary where they can understand their own pain and share it at their own pace.

Eldredge believes, as do others such as Robert Bly, that men have experienced deep wounds, usually at the hands of their fathers. Eldredge explains that every boy grows up with a need to believe that he has a "dangerous capacity to really come through." A boy's passage into manhood involves many of these moments, and the father's role is to arrange them and to invite the boy into them. He must "keep an eye out for moments when the question arises [Am I enough?] and then speak into the son's heart, *yes you are*. You have what it takes. And that is why the deepest wound is always given by the father."[3]

Several years ago, I attended a workshop called Finding Father God. It was a powerful experience. It was not intended solely for men, but because of an inner urging, many men came out of the woodwork to attend. In this Saturday event we heard about the love the Father has for us. Together we studied, prayed, sang, and embraced one another as we meditated upon the healing Scripture, "How great is the love the Father has lavished on us, that we should be called children of God!" (1 John 3:1). Many of us had heard time and again the need for a saving relationship with Jesus Christ. But to hear anew that the Father has lavished love on us, and that we could bask in that love, was tremendously healing.

I remember looking around the auditorium in Portland, Oregon, and seeing men lay hands on men, tears flowing easily, and father wounds being healed. At first the experience seemed awkward—men engaged in deep encounters with other men—possibly even contrived, but most participants seemed to settle into this healing community. I remember feeling excited that the church had moved into the healing realm of men's pain. Cautiously I allowed someone to pray for me and my own father issues. This was a day when the church had mined new territory and had struck gold.

Men will attempt to dance around the deep issues, but if they are led, they often will follow. If they are to heal completely, they must face the losses they have experienced at the hands of their mothers and, more importantly, their fathers. The leaders in the church are learning more about these issues and are leading the way.

Men must go deep with other men who have been there and know the terrain. They must, if possible, do the work with other men, especially their fathers. Father-son healing is what we ultimately seek.

Are leaders and mentors available? Such people are hard to find, but thankfully, they are out there. Men within the church have been excited about Eldredge's work and are ready for the next step.

The Balanced Man

As you read the list above, you may have wondered what it has to do with men and the blues.

It has everything to do with men and the blues because the unbalanced man is the one who suffers most from buried pain and unmet hopes and desires. The *unconscious man,* unaware of his needs and the need for a balanced life, is most likely to succumb to the darkness of profound discouragement and depression.

The balanced man is able to experience and deal with the gamut of feelings. He is able to be present to all of life. He knows how to handle the depths of discouragement and the heights of joy. As Carroll and Dyckman state in *Chaos or Creation*,

> In a healthy individual, feelings constantly change— from anger to love, sadness or joy. Each feeling indicates the individual's personal response to the environment. Each directly expresses the life forces within the person. This is precisely what the depressed person is unable to do: express feeling.[4]

The balanced man not only expresses his feelings but also develops his faith. I am reminded of the quintessential work on disciplines of faith by Richard Foster, *Celebration of Discipline*. Foster outlines many of the disciplines of the mature disciple of Christ. He discusses the many aspects of mature faith, including, but not limited to, prayer, fasting, meditation, study, and worship. The mature and balanced man has undoubtedly incorporated many of these disciplines into his life.

The balanced man. A man in touch with his feelings. A man who knows his faith and is comfortable with related questions that inevitably arise. He does not need to control God or others with his faith. He lives with ambiguity at times. Surely this man is hard to find. Surely we are asking for the moon now, right?

Where do we find a man who is able to effectively create adventure, rein in his passions and secure them for his wife, and also locate and embrace his right livelihood? Where is the man who finds time for affiliation with other men while also paying attention to his deeper needs for healing? Where is the man who will pursue God—at times through prayer, at times through fasting, at times though meditation and study?

I will be the first to say that this man is, indeed, hard to find. We have few guides in this kind of balancing act. In fact, your man may have to find his own way because the lack of leaders, both spiritual and secular, is so severe. But this should not stop you or him from asking God to raise up men who will lead men on the healing journey.

A Different Path

In a world with so few "real men," Sam stood out. He began his ministry playing a bit part as youth pastor in a church I attended in the mid 90s. He has since become a senior pastor. Jovial yet unpretentious, Sam was "the real deal," and he dared to be different.

Sam was about 30 years old when I met him, happily married with two young children. Things hadn't always been rosy for him. He often talked about a time when he was far less clear about his life's direction. He had to change his course because he was on a fast track to hell.

Sam told of growing up in a hardworking professional family. He was the middle of three children. He talked about how his parents, particularly his father, expected Sam to follow him in either the law profession or some other high-paying career.

But when Sam was growing up, he rarely saw his father. Sam was not interested in a job that demanded 70-plus hours a week and made him a stranger to his own children. Sam's passions were in writing and reading. He always hoped to be a writer, though his parents never encouraged him to pursue this path.

"Writers are nothing more than starving artists," his father would chide. Needless to say, the bond between Sam and his father was fragile and in need of repair.

Sam's older brother became "the responsible one," attending college and establishing himself in a legal career. Sam's younger sister was rebellious in high school but straightened out her life and is, as of this writing, happily married and living in the same community as Sam and her parents. She graduated from college and is a teacher.

Sam decided he was going to walk a different path. He would not follow the obligatory corridor to college or into the "golden handcuffs" of responsible employment. He chose a meandering road that included writing poetry, travel, and studying abroad. He developed a love for people of Third World countries after spending time in Mexico and Central America. It was there that he studied the Bible and developed a heart for mission work.

In spite of its limitations, an obligatory path offers security. Men know what is expected of them. They know how to behave, what to do, and where their path will lead. A solid identity will emerge, and a career trajectory will include pay raises, and, eventually, a middle-management job with even more benefits.

Next come the wife and two-plus children. The kids will attend public school and grow up in suburbia. The family will attend church, take on a leadership role here and there, participate in the PTA and perhaps on the church board. These roles serve as anchors for the "average" family.

But Sam did not want that life. He dared to carve out his own niche, separate from the one his family expected. This winding existence of a vagabond was rewarding, though he did long for more anchors. After a few years, he finally entered college and studied theology. In the process, he began to serve the church and found in the ministry a way to serve the Lord while retaining his freedom and individuality.

Sam entered the ministry with a need to reclaim anchors he had lost in his past. He had wandered around and was now ready to settle down. The senior pastor, who had taken a liking to Sam, offered him the job as youth pastor. He appreciated Sam's wit and his enthusiasm for kids and missions. Sam had made a decision to serve the Lord and build a new life. Through the church, he met his wife, and together they decided to give their lives in service to God.

Although Sam was several years younger than me when we met, he taught me a great deal about being a man in the church. Something was special about him: He was excited, unique, determined, and internally directed. He did not need approval from others. He was not on a path to make a million dollars. He just wanted to love the Lord, be faithful to his wife and family, and have fun. He was able to do all three with gusto.

Most importantly, Sam had done a lot of internal work, specifically attending to the wound between himself and his father. He had spent many hours talking with his father about the message he received about acceptable performance. Sam shared the pain he carried as a result of not being able to garner his father's approval because of his desire to work with words and people. Sam also asked for forgiveness for the resentment he had carried against his father and the secret rebellion he had acted out toward him. They shared several poignant healing moments and now enjoy a restored relationship.

Sam's maturity showed in the way he conducted himself as a man. He had no need to be "macho." He was comfortable with his emotions. He could share his pain and his joy with family and friends. He could also sympathize with others' sorrows. Sam seemed comfortable mentoring other men who were dealing with their father wounds and their struggles with addictions and depression. He was comfortable with his faith and was able to share it in a way that was not "preachy." The church will become more and more effective as more spiritual leaders like Sam provide mentoring, modeling, and compassion for Christian men.

A Healing Community of Men and Women

The church is you and I. It is a common gathering of men, women, and children. As such, it can be whatever we desire it to be. If we want to make it a healing community, a place where ragamuffins are as welcome as princes and princesses, we can do so.

How can women, working within the structure of the church, help men achieve a balanced life that is free of the blues? That is the fundamental question. Again, I would like to challenge you to consider how you can help.

First, *the church can help men by speaking honestly to them.* Many of us have a tendency to wink and laugh or use sarcasm to say that we are really tired of men being underdeveloped emotionally and spiritually. Now is the time to speak honestly and to tell men the truth.

You can begin this in your home by talking with your man so that he can begin to listen. (See the Seven Cs mentioned earlier in this book.) You can avoid winking in the face of his immaturity. You, along with the church, can be vigilant about not enabling bad behavior.

Second, *you can tell him the truth about his need to take responsibility for his problems.* Sadly, many problems need attention. We all know what taking responsibility looks like. We also know what avoidance looks like. We know this from watching our children dance and weave in the face of trouble. We watch them use all kinds of "thinking errors," such as making excuses, rationalizing, denial, and other tactics to avoid facing their destructive patterns.

Thinking errors don't merely cause depression. They also are the barriers that prevent men from growing out of the blues. They are the patterns that result when your church refuses to tell it the way it is. When your church laughs about men's bad behavior, say something to the pastor. Sarcasm and teasing are not options if you are to say clearly, concisely, and with conviction that something must change.

Third, *gather the people.* A community of believers is powerful. It can exert a powerful influence upon men if it will dare to. The community could agree, for example, to circle around the man and share their concerns. They could strongly encourage him to get help for his depression. They could confront him about the behaviors, such as work or alcohol addiction, that reinforce the depression.

"Yes, but he would hate me for putting him on the spot." Possibly. But by failing to speak out, you relegate yourself and him to a life of misery that together you could change with the help of a few faithful warriors. Provide a safe place where he could feel understood, not shamed.

Fourth, *encourage your church to provide more teaching about the issues addressed in this book.* Talk to your men's ministry leader. Bring in experts who will speak with conviction and compassion. Dare to address issues pertaining to emotions, wounds, and sexuality that are typically swept aside. Encourage your pastor to create forums where men have an opportunity to talk straight with one another. It can happen.

Some time ago I heard that the alternative church I referred to earlier held a Saturday forum to talk about sexual sins. Although I did not attend, word quickly spread through the community that when a few dared to confess, others followed. It was the first of many forums designed to help men quit talking above the issues, put on their hip boots, and enter the pond. It was a healing experience for the men and an encouragement to me to see that they could come together to share honestly in the right format.

This unique church, and others like it, is beginning to meet men's needs. I am hopeful that other churches will follow in its footsteps. I am hopeful that the larger church will begin to honestly confront the issues we face on a daily basis. I am hopeful that, out of necessity, we will take off our masks and make ourselves truly available, offering our gifts to minister to one another.

When we are willing to do that, male depression and many other problems will be resolved.

chapter 10

The Healing, Life-Giving Community

Carry each other's burdens, and in this way you will fulfill the law of Christ.

—GALATIANS 6:2

As I STEPPED OUTSIDE THE FRONT DOOR of our room into the bright Costa Rican sunlight, I was immediately greeted by a middle-aged American named Brent. He was cleaning the pool near our room. This tall, tanned man, sporting shoulder-length blond hair with a hint of gray, engaged me in small talk that eventually led to him sharing how he had packed up everything he owned and moved to Costa Rica.

He and his wife had lived in Hawaii, where they'd spent nearly 20 years running a hotel. They had raised a family and sent their children off to college. One day, according to Brent, he got tired of the rising taxes and decided he'd had enough. In an impetuous moment, they sold their belongings, packed up what was left, and moved to Costa Rica, never pausing to look back. They now run a bed and breakfast near one of the most famous beaches in Costa Rica.

Brent shared enough to pique my curiosity. How did they manage to give up everything they were familiar with and move to a foreign country? Had he been frightened of such a move? Had the adventure been what they'd expected?

As I showered him with my pedantic queries, he grinned. By his wry smile, I could tell that people often asked these questions. "Many people come here and see the beauty, the idyllic setting, and think about selling it all like we did and moving down here. They rush off to a Realtor and start making arrangements to buy a lot. They don't wait until they get home to think it over. They don't count the cost."

"What cost?" I asked. I looked again at his sparkling adobe home and the swimming pool in front. It appeared to be a pretty sweet life to me.

"Well, does your family live down here? Are your friends here? Do you enjoy your work? If your family doesn't live here, and you like them, don't move here. If you have friends that you enjoy, and they don't live here, don't move here. If you have an occupation and like the people you work with, don't move here. You need those people in your life."

I stared at him, wondering how he had become so wise. It had to be the Costa Rican sun.

"'If your family doesn't live here, and you like them, don't move here.' That's good advice," I said.

Brent's counsel was similar to the advice that I have given throughout this book. His words provided a context for some of the truths I've already mentioned. We need one another. That especially applies to the man who struggles with the blues. Isolation is a killer.

Community. Those people, family, friends, and acquaintances that give our lives meaning. We take it for granted. Yet, when it's threatened, even by haphazard schemes of moving to tropical climes, we may be asking for trouble. Our community offers advice, engages in creative conversation, and adds history and perspective to our lives. The members of our community know us and relate to us in ways that strangers cannot.

Koinonia Community

This final chapter will reinforce critical truths, one of which is certainly the value of community. Few people understand the importance of fending off isolation through community.

The Bible contains a unique example of community that some people still follow today in various ways. Acts 2:42-47 tells how the early church gathered in community:

> They devoted themselves to the apostles' teaching and to the fellowship, to the breaking of bread and to prayer.... All the believers were together and had everything in common. Selling their possessions and goods, they gave to anyone as he had need....They broke bread in their homes and ate together with glad and sincere hearts, praising God and enjoying the favor of all the people.

Who of us has not wondered if this could really work? Could we really live like that, in a community where we looked out for one another? Where we shared what we had, without concern for greed and accumulation? Without wondering if our neighbor had more goodies stockpiled than we did?

The passage is clear. They lived in real community with one another, and it worked. They cared about one another in a way that Brent alluded to. We are connected to one another, and that connection is vital to our well-being. Research has long shown that those who are well-connected are healthy, and those who are not well-connected do not fare as well.

Koinonia—fellowship with one another—was a good thing not only for early Christians. It can be a good thing for us as well.

I am sure we would all agree that not all communities are healthy, life-giving bodies. So what is a healthy community?

Life-Giving Community

As we travel the streets of Costa Rica, we share a common salutation or expression when leaving another's company. *"Pura vita! Pura vita!"* This is the walking pronouncement of the Costa Ricans. As I write this chapter I am vacationing in this beautiful country.

Pura vita. The literal translation is "pure life." But to the Ticos, as Costa Ricans call themselves, it generally means "good wishes," or even "chill, take it easy." As I arrive at my hotel to rent a room, they greet me with *"pura vita."* When I leave, they shout *"pura vita."*

Costa Rica is a beautiful, lush, and verdant land. If anyone can say *"pura vita"* with conviction, the Ticos can. Relaxation appears to come naturally to them. They seem to appreciate the land, which offers so much bounty. The hills are fecund with coffee plants, pineapple plantations, banana trees, and almost every other tropical fruit-bearing plant imaginable. And why not? After all, this is a Costa Rica—"Rich Coast."

As I reflect upon their greeting and send-off, I realize that *pura vita* is perhaps what we are all searching for. It is what the depressed man and woman want and seek. It is what the discontented ones travel the earth searching for. It is what the stressed-out housewife wants; it is what the irritable and tired man wants; it is what the needy want more than anything. Pure life. Certainly, pure life is antithetical to the vapid existence of the depressed man. Somewhere along the way, pure life has drained from him like liquid from a container with a hole in it.

Thankfully, as we bring this book to a close, we find hope for the man with the blues and for you, the woman who loves him. We find hope as we consider living a pure life in community, for this is where we find happiness. It is in community, in our mingling with spouse, family, friends, church, and larger society, that we truly experience life. Community is a powerful antidote to male depression that we dare not neglect.

Pure Life

Does *pura vita* mean the same thing to you as it means to the Ticos? Is it something esoteric, vague, and unreachable? Does it have any usefulness in a book about male depression? I think so.

We cannot read the gospels without getting a clear sense that Jesus wanted, more than anything, to offer pure life. Pure, unadulterated, life. And He offered it through community—relational community with Him and others in our world. Jesus asked the ones with full hands to empty them so that He could offer them *pura vita*. He challenged the ones with lifestyles so full they could hardly add another material weight to let it all go in favor of *pura vita*. He challenged the ones stressed about tomorrow to let go and live fully in this day.

Pure life, especially as Christ taught it, should be rife with exuberance and satisfaction.

Why should pure life imply happiness? Several reasons come to mind.

First, pure life implies an absence of the impurities that tend to clutter our lives. These impurities, or sins, only bring us unhappiness and conflict. Christ came to offer us life, free from the bondage to sin (Romans 8:9).

Second, a pure life implies a life of abundance. The Beatitudes (Matthew 5) offer a straightforward prescription for blessings in our lives. Jesus does not promise us material wealth, but He assures us of abundant comfort and mercy. He tells us we will inherit the kingdom of God. This life, while not without difficulties, is filled with joy and gladness.

Third, a pure life implies focus. As Christians, we can understand our spiritual gifts and act within them. We can use our gifts to bless others and experience joy. We can use our gifts to bless the body of Christ. We can participate in Kingdom living and saving a lost world.

Fourth, a pure life, from a Christian perspective, gives us an eternal view, one that helps us cope with everyday struggles and offers us life everlasting. With this eternal point of view, we can experience peace. We know in our hearts that "in all things God works for the good of those who love him, who have been called according to his purpose" (Romans 8:28).

Finally, pure, effervescent living is part and parcel of any healing community, and that is what I want to discuss in depth in this chapter. Pure, joyful life should emanate from any healing community and should help its members to live with these blessings:

- clarity
- goodness
- depth
- health in mind, soul, and emotions
- community
- fellowship with God

Certainly we could consider many more benefits of pure life and the healing community. But let's consider these in greater depth.

Living with Clarity

As I have previously stated, the pure life is not one that is cluttered with "fillers." It is not stuffed with things that fill our lives but don't add meaning. Take a moment to look around, and you will see people who have filled their lives with events, work, and many other "things" as a way of convincing themselves that they are truly living.

Karl and Kathy were a 40-year-old couple who came to see me at her insistence. Their story is one I have heard many times, and perhaps you will quickly recognize the theme as one we have seen previously in this book.

Karl was vague about why they had come to see me. "My wife said that we should talk to someone," he said.

"But why does she want to see someone, Karl?" I asked. Kathy waited for him to answer, but Karl seemed genuinely puzzled.

Finally, he let it out. "She says that I'm too busy with my work and hobbies to spend any quality time with her."

"What do you think about that, Karl?"

"I disagree. Sure, I work hard, but it's so I can give my family things that my father never gave us kids." There it is again. Compensation for the father wound.

"It's not just that you work so hard," Kathy said. "It's what happens even when you are with us. You're there in body, but your mind is someplace else. Even when you're not at work, you're thinking about work or one of your projects."

"So, tell me about your life," I said. "How much do you work? What do you do when you leave the job?"

Karl went on to tell me, grudgingly and indirectly, what so many men say. They work too hard, collect too many toys, and busy themselves in any manner of ways so they don't have to communicate with their families. All the while, their kids grow up and their wife occupies herself with other matters. The marriage dies. And the man becomes depressed because he is so focused on things that distract him from the pure life.

As Karl talked about his life, he began to see that his activities were like carbohydrates—plenty of filler but not particularly nutritional. He could see that his life was crammed with activities, but in his heart he was far less than satisfied. In time, he was able to see, through the help of his small community— his wife and children—that he needed more focus in his life and that his family was central to that focus.

Living with Goodness

As we see from looking into Karl's life, we can easily become preoccupied. Perhaps the greatest tragedy of filling a life with activities, as good as they might appear to be, is that they choke out real goodness. So what do we mean by real goodness? Several Scriptures will give us a better understanding.

"The fruit of the Spirit is love, joy, peace, patience, kindness, goodness, faithfulness, gentleness and self-control. Against such things there is no law. Those who belong to Christ Jesus have crucified the sinful nature with its passions and desires" (Galatians 5:22-24). Paul makes it clear that life is more than what we can see, touch, and feel. It includes the life of the Spirit. This life, available to all, is separate from the desires of the flesh that create problems for us.

To one church Paul says, "Set your minds on things above, not on earthly things" (Colossians 3:2). To another he says, "Those who live in accordance with the Spirit have their minds set on what the Spirit desires" (Romans 8:5). What a practical piece of wisdom for a pure life. From our thoughts come intentions, good and bad, which give rise to actions. A life emanating from the Spirit will be filled with goodness.

Most churches have groups that exist for the purpose of doing good. These groups minister to the poor by visiting those in nursing homes and serving meals to the disenfranchised. Missionaries dedicate themselves to building churches in Third World countries. Whether the call is about meeting physical, emotional, or spiritual needs, goodness is the result, according to the gospel. In the process, not only the recipients but also the givers are blessed.

What a wonderful breath of fresh air this message can be for those who struggle with the blues. Life in the Kingdom transcends that which we experience in our physical bodies. The man with the blues must step out and serve others. In this way, he will be blessed himself. He must practice doing good. This is yet another gift of healthy community living. We heal the community, and by doing so, the community heals us.

Living Deeply

Pure life, one that sustains us and enriches us, goes deep. In a world dominated by superficiality and fast things, going slowly and deeply runs against the grain.

Aristotle said the unexamined life is not worth living. The Scriptures exhort us to explore the thoughts and intentions of the heart. They encourage us to explore our motives, to know what is happening inside us at a deeper level.

I once spent a weekend at a Franciscan renewal center. While there, I spent my time in solitude—reading, resting, praying. I also arranged to meet with a nun who was trained as a spiritual director.

As I approached her simple office at our prearranged time, I was unsure what would take place. I was unclear about what a spiritual director did.

As I sat down, she offered a kind greeting and then asked what I wanted to talk about. I had decided to focus on questions of faith—specifically, how to know more about God and His love for me. I asked the nun how she experienced God and His love.

The elderly woman jumped out of her chair and pointed to the budding cherry trees on the property. She then pointed to the sky and the birds flying overhead. "Do you see that? How can you look around and see the hand of God everywhere and not feel His love? How can you smell the sweet fragrance of spring and not feel the touch of God? Do you notice these things? Do you take time to see what is around you? Do you take the time to thank the Creator for His wonderful blessings?"

As a matter of fact, I was in the habit of taking those things for granted. I was in such a hurry that I did not reflect on God's gifts to me and His children. When she called my attention to them, I was moved.

I went back to my room and journaled about the experience. I noted the tremendous gifts that God was giving me and others who believed in Him. I also was thankful for the nun's ability to share these gifts with me by calling my attention to them. In our small two-person community, she challenged me to participate in an attitude of awareness and gratitude as a way of worshipping God.

Living Well: Spirit, Soul, and Bodies

We function as total beings. We cannot separate our spiritual nature from how we tend to our bodies, or our physical nature from how we think and care for our minds.

God calls us to be good stewards of our bodies.

We often eat our meals in community. We eat together as a family, with friends, or in a larger gathering place, such as a church. This pattern was established in the early church. Believers gathered to break bread, to pray, and to share fellowship. Something is healing about being connected to one another in pursuits that involve sharing a meal or perhaps studying the Scriptures.

I have been impressed in recent years with the movement in the church to pay closer attention to our physical well-being, knowing it impacts our spiritual well-being. For example, some churches offer classes that call attention to proper nutrition and the important role it plays in emotional and spiritual health. Many churches have nurses who tend to the physical needs of their parishioners.

The church has always provided wonderful opportunities for spiritual study, but we can offer even more opportunities to participate in discussions on physical and emotional health. I am encouraged when I see churches offer classes that support those experiencing divorce or significant loss. My church recently offered a class on how setting boundaries can impact emotional and spiritual health.

John is the pastor of spiritual formation at our church. He is a soft-spoken man with a ready smile and kind greeting. He is excited about offering ways to experience the Christian faith in atypical formats that involve many senses in a community setting. We might listen to the Word, read, sing, or say a prayer together by candlelight. We might kneel, raise hands, or bow in reverence. He is a spiritual guide who uses experiences that are often new to us but that ignite our minds, wills, and emotions in a community setting. The experience is like a soothing balm to the weary, disheartened soul.

Living Within Community

We all live in community, right? Well, yes and no. Certainly we live near a community, or perhaps even in a community. But not everyone lives *within* their community.

Our life in relation to our community is a critical issue, especially for the man with the blues. Our identity is partially based upon our network of relationships. This is our community. Our community consists of those people with whom we identify, the ones we call in times of celebration and despair. These are the people who know us, and we know them. They define us and we define them.

Many of us live fragmented lives. Currently, I am more fragmented than at other times of my life. Because I am in transition, moving from one locale to another, my roots are not as deep as I would like them to be. I am forming new friendships and becoming active in a new church. This is an anxious time because I usually enjoy living actively within my community. At this time, my community, those with whom I am deeply connected, exists partially in my old city and partly in my new one. This time of transition is uncomfortable. Perhaps you can understand.

We fare better—emotionally, spiritually, and physically— when we are not only in a community but also living within the fabric of that community. Knowing that friends are ready and willing to pray for us at a moment's notice is a reassuring thing indeed. And reaching out to help others, setting aside our everyday issues, is a way to move beyond the tyranny of the urgent in our own lives.

How is the strength of the fabric of your community? Are you living *in* a community, or *within* your community?

Pure life involves living with people with whom you can truly relate. People to whom you are attached. Those relationships go deeper than Sunday morning greetings. Pure life includes the celebratory dinner table, joking with friends, pouring out your heart in a soft and quiet moment. This connection is sadly lacking in the depressed man's life. But you can help him find it again.

Pure life within community makes you feel connected, embraced, and escorted through life. This is incredibly powerful for all of us but even more so for the man with the blues.

Living Close to God

Hildur was a dear, elderly woman, a Swedish emigrant who spoke with a strong accent that was sometimes hard to understand. Short and a bit plump, she had a contagious smile and a warm embrace. She was not shy about her faith.

I had the privilege of spending a lot of time around Hildur as I grew up in the Swedish Covenant Church. She was always at the heart of the frequent socials and made her home a place of hospitality. You know the kind of home I'm talking about—where you don't have to worry about what you touch or whether or not you've wiped your feet.

At the Sunday dinner table, she always arranged a feast fit for a king. But more important than the food was the conversation about what had taken place during the church service a few hours before. She wanted to know how the sermon had touched our hearts and what we were going to do about it. She wanted to know if we were living close to God and letting Him touch our lives.

I was always impressed that Hildur shared her faith with her community—as naturally as she shared her roast beef. She did it not only on Sundays but every day of the week. Hildur lived close to God and could not help but express her faith to all she met. She never pushed her faith on me, but she shared it freely and asked me what I thought about spiritual matters. I felt very close to her for several formative years of my life.

Pure life, vibrant life, cannot be separated from living close to God. I do not believe a person can have a joyful life without a vibrant faith. Many people neglect this aspect of their lives and need to refuel it to keep it alive. Those who experience the blues have often either neglected their faith or felt discouraged and distanced from God.

Not long ago, I asked my aging mother how her faith had changed over the years. I had always sensed her strong faith, and it had been an inspiration to me. My mother cited words from the apostle Paul that have also been popularized in a hymn:

"For I know whom I have believed, and am persuaded, that he is able to keep that which I have committed unto him against that day" (2 Timothy 1:12 KJV).

I will never forget that moment. Her response reminded me again of my faith legacy, that community of believers that cared about my spiritual development. The people in that old church on the corner of Forest and Champion Street cared about my walk with the Lord. They wanted me to grow in my spiritual life. That is faith community at its best.

Living Water

In the gospel of John, we read of an encounter Jesus had with a Samaritan woman. The Jews and Samaritans hated one another, so this conversation was remarkable. I am fond of the story because this unlikely friendship includes a metaphor of pure life—living water.

You might recall that Jesus was passing through Samaria and was tired from His journey. He sat down by a well, and a Samaritan woman came to draw water. Jesus asked her for a drink. Given the traditional national animosities, this was an unusual act.

The woman recognized the awkwardness of the moment and said, "You are a Jew and I am a Samaritan woman. How can you ask me for a drink?"

Jesus replied, "If you knew the gift of God and who it is that asks you for a drink, you would have asked him and he would have given you living water" (John 4:9-10).

A Jew asking a Samaritan for a drink? Him telling her that she should have asked for living water? I'm sure she found this very perplexing.

Jesus goes on to explain Himself. "Everyone who drinks from this water will be thirsty again, but whoever drinks the water I give him will never thirst. Indeed, the water I give him will become in him a spring of water welling up to eternal life."

Still, this could not have turned on any light switches for the woman. Jesus was saying that from within, a spring of pure, living water can flow. How can this be? How can one acquire this spring of water that will lead to eternal life? This, of course, is the gospel—the good news.

Besides the fact that Jesus broke racial barriers by asking for a drink from a Samaritan and later spoke about her multiple marriages, this passage is remarkable for what it tells us about the living water that can spring up within and lead to eternal life. This comes from a relationship with the living Lord.

The man bowed down by the blues is terribly thirsty. He has experienced his own version of the "dark night of the soul" spoken of by St. John of the Cross. He has felt depleted and withered by life's circumstances. He is living in a parched land, perhaps a parched community, desperately in need of new life. He needs living water, the kind that springs up from within. This is another aspect of the healing community, for that community helps the depleted one find living water.

Imagine living water that springs from within. Pure, living water. In a day when all seems to be tainted by the dirtiness of life, pure water is very appealing.

But we bump into a problem. Just as the Samaritan woman was befuddled and confused by the words of Jesus, we will be too if we try to understand this passage intellectually. It makes no sense to the rational mind. Water rising up from within a person? Nonsense!

But if we turn off the rational mind and allow the message to speak to our spiritual mind, something else happens. If we ask the Spirit of God to reveal what this passage can say to us today, something quite miraculous can take place. I can imagine the Word of God acting as leaven within me, creating a purity of life that rises up and cleanses my inner being. I can imagine living water taking the place of the "fillers" that clutter my inner being.

Can you imagine this happening in your life? Can you imagine your discouraged and depressed man meditating on this passage and enjoying a cold, pure drink of water from within? And can you imagine the impact this water could have on a parched soul?

Jesus often performed miracles, and large numbers of listeners came to partake of His message. However, His words were sometimes hard to understand or follow, and some people slipped away. At one poignant moment, people were abandoning the cause, and Jesus asked His disciples if they too wanted to leave. Peter, like us, reflected on his options and then said, in my opinion, the wisest thing he ever spoke.

"Lord, to whom shall we go? You have the words of eternal life. We believe and know you are the Holy One of God" (John 6:68-69).

The Church as a Healing Community

The church can be at the heart of a healing community. God has entrusted the church with the preaching of His Word, which has power to change lives. God's Word is not just a collection of principles or statement of values. Paul understood the gospel

to be a living thing, "bearing fruit and growing" in the Colossian
believers (Colossians 1:6). The writer to the Hebrews testified
that the Word of God is "living and active…it judges the
thoughts and attitudes of the heart" (Hebrews 4:12). Peter's
preaching "cut to the heart" of his hearers (Acts 2:37). He had
heard firsthand Jesus' "words of eternal life" (John 6:68). Who
knows what might spring to life when God plants the seed of
His Word in the heart of a depressed man?

The church also offers people the incredible opportunity
to experience the life-giving ministry of the Spirit. Jesus promised that He would be with even "two or three" who gather in
His name (Matthew 18:20). Think of what this means. Just as
God breathed life into Adam through His Spirit, He breathes
life into believers today (see Genesis 2:7; John 20:22; Acts 1:8;
2:4). When life seems hopeless, we need to remember that hope
is always available. "Flesh gives birth to flesh, but the Spirit gives
birth to spirit" (John 3:6). "The Spirit gives life; the flesh counts
for nothing. The words I have spoken to you are spirit and they
are life" (John 6:63). As the faith community shares the life of
the Spirit, people who are spiraling downward can experience
a miracle of transformation. "Now the Lord is the Spirit, and
where the Spirit of the Lord is, there is freedom. And we, who
with unveiled faces all reflect the Lord's glory, are being trans-
formed into his likeness with ever-increasing glory, which comes
from the Lord, who is the Spirit" (2 Corinthians 3:17-18).

Anyone who immerses himself in the spiritual life of a
vibrant Christian community also finds encouraging examples
of men and women who have grown through difficult circumstances. Thankfully, the façade of church families who live
a perfect life and never struggle is crumbling. In its place we see
real people confessing sins, asking for forgiveness, looking for

direction and encouragement, and reaching out in love to help one another. Many churches are developing men's programs that dare to address thorny issues, such as the temptations men face. Churches also offer support to family members as well.

This community of "wounded healers" can offer a helpful blend of support and accountability. In the church we find love, acceptance, and forgiveness. We experience the strengthening grace we need for real change. But we also receive direction and guidance to make sure that we experience that change in our everyday lives. This is not a place for mere sympathy. The church is a group of people who are committed to "become mature, attaining to the whole measure of the fullness of Christ" (Ephesians 4:13). This growth includes learning to accept responsibility for our own lives.

"Carry each other's burdens, and in this way you will fulfill the law of Christ" (Galatians 6:2). A proper interpretation of this passage suggests that we are to assist others with burdens that *they cannot carry on their own.*

Tamara was a 35-year-old woman who came to me complaining that her husband was becoming more withdrawn, irritable, and in her opinion, depressed. She admitted that she was not an expert in diagnosing depression, but she was concerned that it might be at the root of their marital problems. Their sex life had dwindled to nothing over the past few years, and she was extremely frustrated. She had made doctors' appointments that he had canceled at the last minute. She had set up meetings with the pastor that he had failed to keep. She had even read about natural remedies, such as St. John's Wort, hoping that they might change his mood. Nothing worked.

When Tamara came to see me, I applauded her heroic efforts to "cure" her husband. However, I asked her who had expended the most energy in his healing. She thought for a nano-second and then smiled. Of course, she had taken on a mission that is common to women and mothers. A problem arises in the house—so fix it. Someone is unhappy—so make him laugh.

But, Tamara protested, what about Galatians 6:2? Aren't we supposed to carry one another's burdens? The answer is yes and no. We are to carry the burdens that others cannot carry for themselves. To carry the ones that they can carry is to enable them, which suggests that they are not capable of solving their own problems. This not only is humiliating to the one being rescued but also creates a sense of helplessness in them. How will they ever become responsible for themselves if we constantly pick up their responsibilities for them?

"So, what can I do?" she asked. We read in Galatians 6:5 that "each one should carry his own load." She should be clear with her husband about what she sees, offer reasonable assistance, and then manage her own life—carry her own load. Show concern, offer helpful suggestions, and then step back. Of course, Tamara feels helpless. She wants to do more. But, as we have learned, Tamara can directly impact only her own life, and that is what she is responsible for.

The Family as a Healing Community

Within the larger community lives the smaller community called the family. We have already talked about the dynamics that occur within a family. Hopefully, you and your man grew up in families that celebrated your arrival. Hopefully, your family provided a safe place to practice new behaviors and ways of being. You were able to experiment with talents, gifts, and assorted personalities. Your family members loved you. They tolerated you and helped you with your moods.

The family that functions properly, as we learned earlier, allows each member a little breathing room, knowing that learning to express and manage moods and even times of depression is part of growing up. The healthy family is big enough to allow for these difficult times. More than once I have heard parents say about their children, "We will get through this and emerge better than before." I have heard wives and husbands share the same sentiments many times about their marital problems.

Of course, this is not always the case. Many people have not found a safety net within their family of origin. They did not find the acceptance and support for their moods and temperaments. They did not find the freedom to try out different "personalities." Instead, they had to behave. They had to conform to the expectation of the most controlling family me mber.

Regardless of how your family was for you, safe or unsafe, freeing or inhibiting, it was your family. Your family, with all its flaws and idiosyncrasies, is yours, and your task, and that of your man, is to make peace with this important community.

Your family can often provide a powerful sense of community that you cannot replicate elsewhere. As we grow older, many of us realize how vital our families are to us and try to reconcile ourselves with their challenges.

For some of us, however, the family has utterly failed to provide the support and encouragement we need. Perhaps your man comes from a family that failed to support and encourage him. Ask yourself these questions:

- Have my spouse and I done everything we can to heal broken family relationships?

- Can my family, or my spouse's, still offer us something, even if it is less than ideal?

- How can my spouse and I foster healthier relationships with our families?

- If our families are destructive to me or my spouse, who can provide the kind of support offered by a healthy family?

Family provides an important connection to others and offers a kind of insulation from the blues. Hopefully, you and your spouse come from families that provide you with a sense of belonging and understanding. If not, perhaps you can promote healing in these relationships. If that is not possible, you may need to grieve this loss and search out those who will agree to serve as "family" to you.

The Embracing Community

True community begins with an understanding that Christ is the head of this gathering. He is the head of the local church and of the larger church community as well.

One day in the temple courts, Jesus engaged in debate over matters of Jewish law. One of the teachers of the law, a Pharisee, asked Him which law was the greatest. Referencing the book of Deuteronomy, He stated that the most important law was "Love the Lord your God with all your heart and with all your soul and with all your mind and with all your strength." However, He did not stop there. He added a most important clause. "The second is this: 'Love your neighbor as yourself'" (Mark 12:29-31). The Pharisee heartily agreed.

However, Luke's account includes the reaction of another religious expert, a lawyer. He knows God's law of love—and he knows that he is unable to fulfill it. But rather than humbly admitting his selfishness and asking Jesus for help, he decides to look for a loophole, a way "to justify himself." So he asks Jesus, "And who is my neighbor?"

Jesus answers with a parable.

> A man was going down from Jerusalem to Jericho, when he fell into the hands of robbers. They stripped him of his clothes, beat him and went away, leaving him half dead. A priest happened to be going down the same road, and when he saw the man, he passed by on the other side. So too, a Levite, when he came to the place and saw him, passed by on the other side. But a Samaritan, as he traveled, came where the man was; and when he saw him, he took pity on him. He went to him and bandaged his wounds, pouring on oil and wine. Then he put the man on his own donkey, took him to an inn and took care of him. The next day he took out two silver coins and gave them to the innkeeper. "Look after him," he said, "and when I return, I will reimburse you for any extra expense you may have (Luke 10:30-35).

This is an amazing story. The religious ones could not soil their hands on the wounded man. Never mind that he was a member of the human race. Never mind that he was wounded and left half dead. The man was certainly suffering, but only the Samaritan reached out to help him.

The priest and Levite saw the wounded, bloody man but passed by on the other side so as to not come too close to him.

I suggest that this story line is not a great deal different from how we treat those with emotional problems. Do we not wish them well, hope that they get the help they need, and then disappear? Do we ever dare to ask deep, personal questions that might be helpful to the depressed person? Do we ever stop to find out if they are getting the help they need, or if we, being neighbors, can help out in some way?

As a psychologist, I am aware that many people do not have adequate health insurance to cover their mental health needs. Furthermore, many cannot afford the medications that could be so helpful in alleviating their debilitating symptoms. Many suffer in silence, partially out of their own pride and embarrassment, because no one stops to ask them the awkward, personal questions that might eventually lead to solutions.

Just a few weeks ago, the pastor of the offshoot church in my hometown scrawled out a check for a man who needed to see me for his depression. The pastor said the man could meet with me as often as was necessary. The man was indebted to the pastor and the church for their obvious neighborliness and kindness.

This church impresses me because they operate like the early church—they give to anyone as they have need. We too, as a church, need to reach out and be neighbors to the depressed men who are suffering alone.

Society as Healing Community

Male depression is a societal problem. It is not just a family problem or a problem for the isolated man. Each member of the community is part of a greater whole. As one struggles, we all struggle. Unless you start out with that premise, you will be like the priest and Levite who pass by on the other side when members of society are wounded, emotionally, spiritually, or physically.

Gospel living has a great deal to say about how we are to relate to one another. Here are a few basic instructions:

- Do not think more highly of yourself than you ought (Romans 12:3).
- Love your enemies (Luke 6:27,35).
- Do not judge others (Luke 6:37).
- Love others (1 Corinthians 13).
- Love the prodigal (Luke 15:11-32).
- Share your spiritual gifts (Romans 12:6-8).
- Engage in fellowship together (Acts 2:44-47).
- Minister the Word (Colossians 3:16).
- Generously give to one another (2 Corinthians 8:7).
- Restore fellow believers and do good (Galatians 6:1-10).
- Submit to one another in love (Ephesians 5:21).
- Bear one another's burdens (Galatians 6:2).

This list could go on and on. We are intertwined with one another. We are to care for one another's needs, bearing the burdens that others cannot bear themselves. This certainly must include men with the blues.

And now we must get practical about how we, as a larger community, can help the man with the blues. I will offer some ideas, and I hope that you will marshal your resources and be creative in helping men who desperately need our help.

- *Education.* One of the first things we can do for the depressed man is to help him understand this is a very treatable illness, assisting him to access the wealth of information currently available. (Many good books are available, online resources abound, doctors often carry helpful pamphlets, and mental health agencies are ready to help.)

- *Support groups* are helpful to those with a variety of problems, such as those suffering from various addictions, loss of a loved one, and depression. Many churches offer wonderful support groups.

- *Medical assistance.* Research has shown that medications, specifically antidepressants, can be particularly helpful in treating depression. We need to ensure that those struggling with depression have access to these medications.

- *Counseling* has proven to be immensely helpful in treating depression. Many different kinds of treatment are available. As a society, we need to be sure that the depressed person has access to counseling services.

- *Spiritual discipleship.* Men who struggle with depression need to be discipled and armed with Scripture. They can also benefit from having someone who will walk with them through the dark times and pray for their healing.

- *Encouragement* from friends and pastors can be very powerful in bringing this problem out of the dark and into the open. Isolation is hurtful. Open honesty is healing.

Create *new opportunities* for friendship and support. As we have said, women can help create relational bridges for men. Watch for chances to engage your man in community activities.

Joining Hands

Picture an olive grove on a balmy moonlit evening. It could be the scene for lovers as they walk hand in hand, gazing into one another's eyes. However, the reality was far from that— nearly as far as humanly possible. The landscape was one of beauty, but the mood was overwhelmingly tragic.

The setting was the Garden of Gethsemane. It was the place Jesus chose to collect His thoughts before His impending death. Interestingly, He did not choose to be alone. He wanted His best friends, His circle of support, to be with Him. Here is the scene as Matthew describes it.

> Then Jesus went with his disciples to a place called Gethsemane, and he said to them, "Sit here while I go over there and pray." He took Peter and the two sons of Zebedee along with him, and he began to be sorrowful and troubled. Then he said to them, "My soul is overwhelmed with sorrow to the point of death. Stay here and keep watch with me" (Matthew 26:36-38).

This is a moment of community at its worst. Our Lord was in utter agony emotionally and spiritually. He took with Him three dear friends with whom He had shared many poignant moments. They had lived intertwined lives for three years. They were, in essence, brothers.

Now, in this dark hour, in anticipation of His tortuous death, Christ asked that His disciples sit and watch with Him. You probably know the rest of the story. They utterly failed Him. Not that we would have done any better, but couldn't they have stayed awake a while with Him? Couldn't they have consoled

Him? Couldn't they have gathered in a circle and prayed for Him? Couldn't they.... The community failed.

Lest we become discouraged, we are not at the end of the story. Yes, the disciples did fail their Friend when He needed them. But Jesus' death includes a resurrection story. So, what is the rest of the story? How does community come through for their beloved Friend?

After the resurrection, their community was reunited. Matthew again records how this happened.

> After the Sabbath, at dawn on the first day of the week, Mary Magdalene and the other Mary went to look at the tomb. There was a violent earthquake, for an angel of the Lord came down from heaven and, going to the tomb, rolled back the stone and sat on it.... The angel said to the women, "Do not be afraid, for I know that you are looking for Jesus, who was crucified. He is not here; he is risen, just as he said. Come and see the place where he lay. Then go quickly and tell his disciples: 'He is risen from the dead and is going ahead of you into Galilee. There you will see him.' Now I have told you." So the women hurried away from the tomb, afraid yet filled with joy, and ran to tell his disciples. Suddenly Jesus met them.

And so the tragic story of community failed becomes a story of community lived out.

Perfectly? No. But the community was intact, and it was very important to our Lord and His friends.

Can you and your larger community do as well? Yes.

Can you help to create a community of support for your man? Yes, of course you can.

Can he do more for himself to create and reinforce the community in which you live? Again, the answer is yes.

Our individual story takes place in community, and the truth is that we need each other. Even as Jesus needed His disciples and family, we too need our friends, family, and larger community. We cannot prevent harm and tragedy from occurring, but we can be available to help in the difficult times. Together we can create a community of love, upholding those who suffer alone from the debilitating effects of depression.

Together, as a caring community, we have hope!

notes

Chapter 1—A Sure and Hidden Darkness: Bringing the Problem into the Light

1. Terrence Real, *I Don't Want to Talk About It* (New York, NY: Scribner Book Co., 1997), 38.

2. Jed Diamond, *Male Menopause* (Naperfille, IL: Sourcebooks Trade, 1998), n.p.

3. Archibald Hart, *Unmasking Male Depression* (Nashville, TN: W Publishing Group, 2001), 29.

Chapter 2—But We Handle Things So Differently! Depression in Women and Men

1. Les Carter and Frank Minirth, *The Freedom from Depression Workbook* (Nashville, TN: Thomas Nelson Publishers, 1995), 7.

2. Archibald Hart, *Unmasking Male Depression* (Nashville, TN: W Publishing Group, 2001), 7.

3. Ronald Levant, *Men and Emotions* (New York, NY: Newbridge Professional Programs, 1997), 2-4.

4. Kathleen Cushman and William Pollack, *Real Boys Workbook* (New York, NY: Villard Books, 2001), 97.

Chapter 3—The Courage to Cry: Defensiveness and Denial

1. Herb Goldberg, *The Hazards of Being Male* (New York, NY: E P Dutton, 1976), 42-43.

2. Robert Hopcke, *Men's Dreams, Men's Healing* (Boston, MA: Shambhala Publications, 1990), 12.

3. John Eldredge, *Wild at Heart* (Nashville, TN: Thomas Nelson Publishers, 2001), 21.

Chapter 4—When Did It Start? Childhood Influences

1. Kathleen Cushman and William Pollack, *Real Boys Workbook* (New York, NY: Villard Books, 2001), 140.

2. Richard Rohr and Joseph Martos, *The Wild Man's Journey* (Cincinnati, OH: St. Anthony Messenger Press, 1992), 89.

3. Herb Goldberg, *The Hazards of Being Male* (New York, NY: E P Dutton, 1976), 12.

4. Sam Keen, *Inward Bound* (New York, NY: Bantam, 1992), 148.

5. Ianla Vanzant, *Up from Here* (San Francisco, CA: HarperCollins Publishers, 2002), 18.

Chapter 5—Working Man's Blues

1. David Burns, *The Feeling Good Handbook* (New York, NY: Plume, 1999), 153.

2. Marva Dawn, *Keeping the Sabbath Wholly* (Grand Rapids, MI: William B. Eerdmans Publishing Company, 1989), 3.

3. Lee Bolman and Terrence Deal, *Leading with Soul* (San Francisco, CA: Jossey-Bass Publishers, 1995), 38.

4. David Whyte, *Crossing the Unknown Sea: Work as a Pilgrimage of Identity* (New York, NY: Riverhead Books, 2001), 132-33.

5. Julia Cameron, *The Artist's Way at Work* (New York, NY: William Morrow and Company, 1998), 194.

Chapter 6—No Buddy's Home: Friendships
1. Richard Rohr and Joseph Martos, *The Wild Man's Journey* (Cincinnati, OH: St. Anthony Messenger Press, 1992), 74-75.
2. Ibid., 85.
3. Ibid., 86.
4. Robert Bly, James Hillman, and Michael Meade, eds., *The Rag and Bone Shop of the Heart* (New York, NY: HarperPerennial, 1992), 119.
5. Ibid., 123.
6. Frank Pittman, *Man Enough* (New York, NY: The Berkeley Publishing Group, 1993), 129-30.
7. Ibid., 165.
8. Ibid., 179.

Chapter 7—Lost in the Woods: Midlife Crisis
1. Robert Bly, *Iron John* (New York, NY: Addison-Wesley Publishing Company, Inc., 1990), 5-6.
2. Gordon Dalbey, *Healing the Masculine Soul* (Waco, TX: Word Publishing, 1988), 75.
3. Ibid., p. 76.
4. Archibald Hart, *Unmasking Male Depression* (Nashville, TN: W Publishing Group, 2001), 170-174.
5. Ibid., 173.
6. Robert Pasick, *Awakening from the Deep Sleep* (San Francisco, CA: HarperSanFrancisco, 1992), 171-72.
7. L. Patrick Carroll and Katherine Marie Dyckman, *Chaos or Creation* (New York, NY: Paulist Press, 1986), 112.
8. Hart, *Unmasking Male Depression,* 175.
9. Carroll and Dyckman, *Chaos or Creation,* 83.

Chapter 8—Walking on Eggshells: Depression and the Family
1. John Bradshaw, *Bradshaw On: The Family* (Deerfield Beach, FL: Health Communications, 1988), 42.
2. Bradshaw, *Bradshaw On: The Family,* 166.
3. Terrence Real, *I Don't Want to Talk About It,* (New York, NY: Scribner, 1997), 303.
4. Bradshaw, *Bradshaw On: The Family,* 42.
5. Ibid., 45.

Chapter 9—The Clarion Cry of the Church
1. John Eldredge, *Wild at Heart* (Nashville, TN: Thomas Nelson Publishers, 2001), 31-32.
2. Ibid., 32-33.
3. Ibid., 68.
4. L. Patrick Carroll and Katherine Marie Dyckman, *Chaos or Creation* (New York, NY: Paulist Press, 1986), 108.